JOHN 1–12
FROM START2FINISH

MICHAEL WHITWORTH

© 2025 by Start2Finish

All rights reserved. No part of this publication may be reproduced, stored in a retrieval system, or transmitted in any form or by any means without the prior written permission of the author. The only exception is brief quotations in printed reviews.

ISBN 978-1-944704-14-8

Published by Start2Finish
Bend, Oregon 97702
start2finish.org

Printed in the United States of America

Unless otherwise noted, all Scripture quotations are from The Holy Bible, English Standard Version®, copyright © 2001 by Crossway Bibles, a publishing ministry of Good News Publishers. Used by permission. All rights reserved.

Cover Design: Evangela Creative

CONTENTS

1.	The Word Became Flesh	5
2.	The First Witnesses	13
3.	Water into Wine	21
4.	Born from Above	29
5.	Living Water	37
6.	Authority of the Son	45
7.	The Bread of Life	53
8.	Division & Decision	61
9.	The Light of the World	69
10.	Seeing & Believing	77
11.	The Good Shepherd	85
12.	Glory Through Grief	93
13.	The Hour Has Come	101

1

THE WORD BECAME FLESH

JOHN 1:1-18

Objective: To understand that Jesus, the eternal Word, became flesh to reveal God's glory, grace, and truth.

INTRODUCTION

A few years ago, scientists captured the first photograph of a black hole—an object so dense that even light cannot escape its pull. The image was haunting: a fiery ring surrounding an inky center where light vanished. For centuries, people stared into the heavens trying to understand what could swallow brightness itself. John begins his Gospel with a far greater mystery—not a black hole that devours light, but a Person who is light.

Before galaxies spun or time began, the Word already existed. John does not start with shepherds or stables but with eternity itself. He wanted his readers to grasp that Jesus did not step onto the stage of history as a late addition; he wrote the script, built the set, and entered the play he authored.

In this lesson, we meet the Word who created all things, the Light who pierces every darkness, and the Son who became flesh to reveal the Father's heart. John's prologue is more than poetry—it's theology that walks and breathes. The eternal God chose to be knowable, touchable, and near. As we explore these verses, we'll learn that understanding who Jesus was before the manger shapes how we follow him long after the cross.

EXAMINATION

The Word in eternity (1:1–2)

Before Bethlehem, before Adam, before the first tick of the cosmic clock—there was the Word. John opens his Gospel with an echo of Genesis 1: "In the beginning." But instead of talking about light and land and livestock, he talked about Logos—the Word. It was John's way of saying that Jesus didn't merely show up in history; he stood outside of it. The Word *was*—not "became." He didn't emerge from the beginning; he already existed when the beginning began.

John goes on to say that "the Word was with God, and the Word was God." Those two phrases dance together without stepping on each other's toes. "With God" suggests distinction; "was God" affirms equality. The Son was not the Father, but he was no less divine. It was as if John anticipated every future heresy and headed them off in twelve Greek words.

The Jewish mind would have remembered "the word of the LORD" as the active agent of creation and revelation. The Greek mind, steeped in philosophy, would have heard "Logos" as the rational principle behind the universe. John pulled both audiences into the same truth: the Logos wasn't an abstract force but a living Person—the eternal Son of God.

The Word and creation (v. 3)

John doesn't linger long in eternity before turning to creation. "All things were made through him, and without him was not anything made that was made." That sentence slams the door on every idea of Jesus as a mere creature. He stood on the Creator's side of the line. Every atom, galaxy, and strand of DNA bears his fingerprints.

John's statement is sweeping—"all things." He left no wiggle room for exceptions. The Word wasn't an assistant to the Creator but the very means of creation. Paul later echoed this truth when he wrote, "By him all things were created … all things were created through him and for him" (Col. 1:16). In other words, Jesus was both the agent and the aim of creation. Everything exists because of him and finds its purpose in him.

It's humbling to realize that the carpenter who fashioned tables in Nazareth once fashioned the stars. The same hands that would one day bear nails had already shaped nebulae.

The Word and life (1:4–5)

"In him was life, and the life was the light of men." John moves from creation to the sustainer of creation. Jesus wasn't just alive; he was *life* itself—the source of physical existence and spiritual renewal. All other life borrowed from him.

Light and life are close companions in John's Gospel. Light reveals; life restores. The "light of men" means that Christ illuminated the meaning of life. Without him, humanity stumbled in the dark, mistaking shadows for reality.

John then adds a line that sounds like thunder against the darkness: "The light shines in the darkness, and the darkness has not overcome it." The verb "shines" is present tense—continuous. The darkness has been punching for millennia, but it has never landed a knockout. Satan could bruise the heel, but he could never snuff the light. The cross looked like midnight, yet even there, light bled through the cracks.

The witness to the Word (1:6–8)

At this point, John introduces another John—John the Baptist—because every light invites testimony. The Baptist was a man sent from God, not a self-appointed influencer. His job description was simple: "to bear witness about the light."

He wasn't the light himself, a clarification that seemed necessary even in his own day. Crowds flocked to him, and some wondered if he might be the Messiah. John deflected the spotlight with joy. Later he said, "He must increase, but I must decrease." The Baptist knew that his calling was to point, not to shine.

In every generation, God has raised up witnesses who stand in that same line of humility. The preacher, teacher, and everyday Christians all echo John's mission—bearing witness that others might believe. The messenger's worth isn't in how bright he glows but in how clearly he points to Jesus.

The true light (1:9–13)

John now turns the focus back to the eternal Son. "The true light, which gives light to everyone, was coming into the world." The "true light" doesn't mean the only light but the genuine one—the standard against which all other lights are measured. Every glimmer of truth or beauty in this world finds its source in him.

Tragically, "the world did not know him." The Creator walked into his own creation, and the tenants didn't recognize the landlord. "He came to his own, and his own people did not receive him." The Jews had centuries of prophetic preparation and still missed him. But before we wag our fingers, we should remember how often we fail to recognize his work in our own lives.

Yet John's Gospel always leaves room for hope. "But to all who did receive him, who believed in his name, he gave the right to become children of God." Faith isn't about pedigree or performance but about receiving and believing. Those who do become part of a new family—not born of blood, "nor of the will of the flesh nor of man, but of God."

John dismantles every notion of salvation by ancestry or effort. Spiritual birth was God's miracle, not man's manufacturing. The same divine Word who spoke the universe into being can speak a new heart into existence.

The Word became flesh (1:14–18)

If John 1:1 is the thunder of eternity, verse 14 is a lightning strike in history: "And the Word became flesh and dwelt among us." The uncontainable God pitched his tent in human skin. The Greek word *eskēnōsen* ("dwelt") literally means "tabernacled." Just as God's glory once filled a portable tent in the wilderness, now it filled a Person in Galilee.

John and the other apostles had seen that glory—"glory as of the only Son from the Father, full of grace and truth." Those two words, grace and truth, summarize God's entire redemptive character. Truth exposes sin; grace covers it. Truth declares the verdict; grace pays the fine. In Jesus, they met and married.

John contrasts this with Moses: "For the law was given through Moses; grace and truth came through Jesus Christ." The law revealed what holiness required but couldn't supply it. Jesus supplied it by embodying it. The law told us what to do; grace tells us what was done.

"No one has ever seen God," John concludes, "but the only God, who is at the Father's side, has made him known." Moses saw God's back; Isaiah saw his train; but in Jesus, humanity saw his face. The Son didn't just resemble the Father—he was God in the flesh. If we want to know what God is like, we look at Jesus.

And that is John's grand introduction: the eternal Word stepped down from infinite glory to finite dust. He spoke galaxies into existence, then learned to speak in a carpenter's shop. He breathed life into Adam, then hung gasping on a cross. The One who was with God and was God became one of us so we might become one with God.

APPLICATION

1. Let his greatness shrink your ego

John's opening lines remind us we are not the main characters. The eternal Word existed before our first breath and will reign long after our last. That truth is not meant to crush us but to free us from self-importance. When we remember that Christ created all things, we stop acting as if the universe depends on our schedule. Worship begins when our gaze shifts from mirrors to Majesty. A healthy dose of "In the beginning was the Word" can deflate any spiritual ego faster than a balloon at a porcupine party.

2. Light still shines in the dark

John said, "The light shines in the darkness." That verb still burns bright in the present tense. Christ's light keeps shining through headlines, heartbreak, and hospital rooms. We cannot always explain the darkness, but we can testify that it never wins. The Word who spoke light into the void now speaks hope into despair. Disciples walk by that light and, like lanterns in a long hallway, carry it forward for others who have lost their way. We do not manufacture the glow—we reflect it.

3. Witness without worrying about credit

John the Baptist teaches modern believers a liberating truth: you can be faithful without being famous. His joy was not in applause but in accuracy—pointing correctly to Christ. When we serve, teach, or encourage, our aim is not visibility but visibility of Jesus. God still sends ordinary people to bear witness in workplaces, schools, and neighborhoods. If our lives quietly direct others to the light, we are succeeding, even if our names never trend. After all, spotlights were made for the stage, not the servants behind it.

4. Receive, believe, and belong

John's prologue offers a stunning invitation: anyone who receives the Son becomes a child of God. Faith is not a prize for the worthy but a gift for the willing. The gospel levels the playing field—no pedigree required. Our culture defines identity by birth certificates and social metrics; John defines it by new birth from God. That means your past no longer dictates your future. To "receive" Christ is not just to accept information about him but to welcome him as Lord. The family resemblance begins when we trust his name and live as those who truly belong.

CONCLUSION

John opens his Gospel by lifting our eyes to eternity and then lowering them to a manger. The eternal Word who created the universe stepped into his own story so we could finally see the Father's face. Grace and truth walked among us, shining light that darkness could not overcome. Every verse of this prologue invites us to worship the One who was before all things and yet became one of us.

In the next section, that light begins to shine publicly. John the Baptist steps forward to identify the Lamb of God, and the first disciples begin to follow. The Word begins to speak—and people start listening.

REFLECTION

1. What does John 1:1–2 reveal about Jesus' relationship to time and creation?

2. How does seeing Jesus as Creator change the way you view your own life and purpose?

3. In what areas of your life do you most need his light to overcome darkness?

4. How does John the Baptist's humility challenge your approach to serving Christ?

5. What does it mean personally for you that the Word "became flesh"?

6. How have you experienced both God's grace and truth through Jesus?

DISCUSSION

1. Why did John begin his Gospel with "In the beginning" rather than with Jesus' birth story?

2. How does John's description of the Word confront modern misunderstandings about Jesus?

3. What are some practical ways believers can "bear witness to the light" today?

4. Why do you think "his own did not receive him," and how does that still happen now?

5. What does it look like to truly "receive" Christ—not just know about him?

6. How does understanding Jesus as both fully God and fully human deepen our faith and worship?

2

THE FIRST WITNESSES

JOHN 1:19-51

Objective: To understand how humble witness and personal invitation reveal Jesus' identity and invite others to follow him.

INTRODUCTION

A few years ago, a reporter interviewed the man who flips the giant "ON AIR" sign outside a popular talk show studio. The reporter expected glamour, but the man just laughed. "I'm not the show," he said. "I just make sure people know when it's starting." That's John the Baptist in a nutshell—the man who knew exactly who he was and who he wasn't.

In this section of John's Gospel, the camera shifts from eternity's heights to the dusty roads of Judea. The eternal Word has arrived, and now the spotlight turns to the first witnesses who recognize him. We meet John the Baptist under interrogation, hear his thunderous cry—"Behold, the Lamb of God!"—and watch as the first disciples leave everything to follow Jesus. Andrew brings his brother Peter; Philip finds Nathanael. The gospel begins to move, one conversation at a time.

This lesson explores the humble faithfulness of John, the unfolding revelation of Jesus' identity, and the contagious excitement of those who first believed. It reminds us that discipleship starts with witness—seeing who Jesus is—and naturally overflows into invitation—helping others see him too. The movement of faith still travels the same path: from beholding to believing, and from believing to bringing.

EXAMINATION

John's interrogation (1:19-28)

If John the Baptist lived today, someone would have built him a website and a podcast. His sermons drew crowds, his baptisms filled the riverbanks, and his wardrobe deserved its own documentary. Word spread fast—from desert to temple—and soon the religious establishment in Jerusalem sent an investigative committee. When popularity rises, scrutiny follows.

The delegation of priests and Levites asked, "Who are you?" It sounded simple enough, but their tone was not curiosity—it was suspicion. They needed to determine whether John posed a theological threat or political problem. The nation had seen self-proclaimed messiahs before, and Rome did not tolerate rival kings.

John did not take the bait. He "confessed and did not deny, but confessed, 'I am not the Christ.'" His clarity is refreshing. Some men spend years trying to be something they're not; John spent his ministry making sure no one confused him for someone greater. When asked if he was Elijah or the Prophet, he answered each with a firm "no." He was not Elijah resurrected, nor another Moses.

Instead, John identified himself in the words of Isaiah 40:3: "I am the voice of one crying out in the wilderness, 'Make straight the way of the LORD.'" In other words, he was the road crew, not the royalty. His ministry was preparatory—leveling the terrain for the coming King.

When the Pharisees pressed him further—"Why then do you baptize if you are not the Christ?"—John replied that his baptism was with water only. His role was external and anticipatory; the One coming after him would baptize with the Spirit. John's humility reached its peak in verse 27: "The strap of whose sandal I am not worthy to untie." In a world where even slaves were spared that menial task, John placed himself below the lowest servant. The man who drew multitudes considered himself unfit to untie the Messiah's shoes.

Behold, the Lamb of God (1:29–34)

The next day, John saw Jesus approaching and proclaimed, "Behold, the Lamb of God, who takes away the sin of the world!" With that single sentence, John connected centuries of sacrifice, prophecy, and longing. The Jewish mind would have raced through the Old Testament: the Passover lamb in Egypt, the daily temple offerings, and Isaiah's suffering servant led like a lamb to slaughter. John's declaration gathered all of it into one Person.

Notice what John did not say. He did not call Jesus "the Lion of Judah," though that was true, or "the King of Israel," though that was coming. He chose "Lamb." The crowd wanted a conqueror; John pointed to a sacrifice. The Lamb came not to crush Rome but to carry sin.

John's witness also clarified his own role. "After me comes a man who ranks before me, because he was before me." Though Jesus' earthly ministry followed John's, his divine existence preceded it. The Baptist confessed that even his ministry of baptism was for the purpose of revealing the Messiah to Israel.

John testified that he had seen the Spirit descend like a dove from heaven and remain on Jesus. That "remain" is key—unlike temporary visitations of the Spirit in the Old Testament, this was a permanent indwelling. The sign confirmed what God had told John in advance: the One upon whom the Spirit descends and remains is the One who baptizes with the Holy Spirit.

So when John said, "I have seen and have borne witness that this is the Son of God," he declared both his experience and his conviction. Faith is never less than evidence—John saw the sign—but it is always more than sight—it is confession.

The first disciples follow (1:35–42)

The next day, John the Baptist again stood with two of his disciples when Jesus walked by. Once more, he said, "Behold, the Lamb of God." The repetition mattered. The Baptist's joy was not in building his own following but in handing them off to Christ. If John's ministry were a relay race, this was the moment he passed the baton.

Hearing their teacher's words, the two disciples—Andrew and, most likely, John the son of Zebedee—followed Jesus. When Jesus turned and asked, "What are you seeking?" it was the first recorded question he spoke in John's Gospel. He did not ask, "Whom are you seeking?" or "Why are you here?" but "What are you seeking?" It was an invitation for self-examination. Every disciple must answer that question sooner or later. Are we seeking comfort, purpose, power—or simply Christ himself?

Their reply, "Rabbi, where are you staying?" revealed both reverence and hunger. They did not merely want an introduction; they wanted time. Jesus responded, "Come and you will see." With those words, the divine Word invited them into fellowship. That simple phrase became a pattern for evangelism: come and see, experience and know.

They stayed with him that day, and whatever they heard or saw changed them permanently. Andrew immediately found his brother Simon and announced, "We have found the Messiah." It's the first explicit confession of Jesus' messiahship in the Gospel. Andrew's joy was too great to hoard; the good news begged for a recipient. Every believer becomes a bridge to someone else.

When Simon met Jesus, the Lord looked at him and said, "You are Simon son of John; you shall be called Cephas" (which means Peter). Jesus not only knew him but renamed him. The Rock had rough edges, but grace saw potential beneath the grit. Christ's first act in Peter's life was to redefine him—not by what he was, but by what he would become.

Philip and Nathanael (1:43-51)

The next day Jesus decided to go to Galilee and found Philip, saying, "Follow me." Philip did and immediately found Nathanael, echoing Andrew's enthusiasm: "We have found him of whom Moses in the Law and also the prophets wrote." Notice the chain reaction—John pointed to Jesus, Jesus called disciples, and disciples brought others. Evangelism in John's Gospel looks less like a marketing strategy and more like word-of-mouth wonder.

Nathanael, ever the skeptic, replied, "Can anything good come out of Nazareth?" The town had a reputation for being small, unrefined, and unimpressive—something like asking if greatness could come from a gas station on Highway 2. Philip didn't argue theology; he simply said, "Come and see." The same invitation Jesus had given now passed through Philip's lips.

When Nathanael approached, Jesus greeted him with insight that pierced to the heart: "Behold, an Israelite indeed, in whom there is no deceit!" Nathanael was stunned. "How do you know me?" Jesus answered, "Before Philip called you, when you were under the fig tree, I saw you."

Whatever Nathanael was doing or praying beneath that tree, Jesus' knowledge of it convinced him completely. He exclaimed, "Rabbi, you are the Son of God! You are the King of Israel!"

Jesus' reply gently teased his newfound faith: "Because I said to you, I saw you under the fig tree, do you believe? You will see greater things than these." Then he added, "Truly, truly, I say to you, you will see heaven opened, and the angels of God ascending and descending on the Son of Man." That image recalled Jacob's ladder in Genesis 28—the link between heaven and earth. Jesus claimed to be the new and living ladder, the true connection between God and man.

The growing chain of witnesses

John 1:19–51 reads like the dawn breaking in slow motion. The light begins to spread—from John's testimony to Jesus' revelation, from disciple to disciple. Each new witness adds another title to the growing list: Lamb of God, Chosen One, Rabbi, Messiah, Son of God, King of Israel, Son of Man. The crescendo builds until readers can no longer doubt who Jesus truly is.

The narrative also reveals the heartbeat of discipleship. Faith starts with hearing someone else's testimony, then becomes personal through encounter. John pointed; Andrew and John followed; Andrew found Peter; Philip found Nathanael. In this chain of witnesses, no one hoarded the truth. The gospel moved person to person, not platform to platform.

And through it all, John the Baptist stood content on the sidelines, watching his own influence wane while Christ's waxed. The voice faded so the Word could be heard. His joy was complete because the Bridegroom had arrived.

John 1:19–51 thus sets the stage for everything that follows. The Lamb has been revealed, the first disciples have been called, and heaven's ladder now stands open. The eternal Word has stepped fully into the world he made—and people have begun to follow.

APPLICATION

1. Know who you are—and who you're not

When the priests asked John who he was, he started by clarifying who he wasn't. That's not false modesty—it's spiritual sanity. Pride often grows in the soil of comparison. But John's humility was rooted in identity. He was a voice, not the Word; a witness, not the light. You and I are called to the same freedom: to serve faithfully without confusing our reflection for the Source. If our lives point others to Christ, we've succeeded, even if our names fade from memory.

2. Behold, not just believe

"Behold, the Lamb of God." Those words are both a command and an invitation. To behold is more than to glance—it's to fix your gaze, to linger, to let wonder do its work. Christianity is not merely believing certain facts about Jesus; it's beholding him with reverent awe. John's testimony reminds us that worship begins with attention. The more clearly we see Christ as the Lamb who takes away sin, the less likely we are to live as if we still carry it.

3. Pass the baton of faith

Andrew, Philip, and the rest did not form a committee to discuss evangelism strategy. They simply found someone they loved and said, "Come and see." True faith can't keep quiet. The gospel moves most powerfully through personal relationships—family members, coworkers, neighbors—people who already trust your voice. You don't need a pulpit; you need proximity. Evangelism isn't about eloquence but enthusiasm. It's less a speech and more a summons to testify to what you've seen.

4. Expect skepticism, answer with invitation

Nathanael's sarcasm—"Can anything good come out of Nazareth?"—echoes in every age. Many dismiss Jesus before meeting him. Philip didn't debate; he invited. "Come and see" remains the best answer to cynicism. Rather than arguing from a distance, we bring people near enough to encounter Christ for themselves. The same Savior who saw Nathanael under the fig tree still sees skeptics under their doubts. He knows them before they know him—and that knowledge changes everything.

CONCLUSION

The opening scenes of John's Gospel introduce not only who Jesus is but also how people come to know him. From John the Baptist's humble witness to the eager faith of Andrew, Peter, Philip, and Nathanael, the light of Christ began to spread through simple, personal testimony. The Messiah had arrived, and hearts were awakening one conversation at a time.

In the next chapter, that light steps into public view. Jesus performs his first sign at a wedding in Cana, transforming water into wine and revealing his glory to the world. The private introductions of chapter 1 give way to a public revelation—showing that the Word who called disciples now begins to display his power.

REFLECTION

1. How did John the Baptist's humility shape the way he carried out his ministry?

2. What does the title "Lamb of God" reveal about Jesus' mission and identity?

3. Why is it significant that the Spirit "remained" on Jesus after his baptism?

4. What does Andrew's eagerness to find his brother teach us about true discipleship?

5. How did Jesus' knowledge of Nathanael demonstrate his divine nature and personal care?

6. Which of the messianic titles in this passage most deepens your understanding of Christ?

DISCUSSION

1. What lessons can we learn from John the Baptist about knowing our role and staying humble?

2. In practical terms, what does it mean for believers today to "behold the Lamb of God"?

3. How can we model Andrew and Philip's "come and see" approach in our own evangelism?

4. What barriers keep people from recognizing Jesus today, and how can we address them graciously?

5. How should Christians respond when friends or family show skepticism like Nathanael's?

6. Why is personal witness—one person sharing with another—still the most powerful way the gospel spreads?

3

WATER INTO WINE
JOHN 2

Objective: To recognize Jesus' transforming power to bring joy and purity—filling what's empty and cleansing what's corrupt.

INTRODUCTION

Years ago, a couple getting married forgot to order enough cake. When the reception crowd realized there weren't enough slices to go around, panic spread faster than frosting. Then an elderly aunt quietly slipped into the kitchen, cut the remaining cake into smaller pieces, and somehow everyone still got a taste. It wasn't a miracle—but it was mercy. She saw a need and stepped in to preserve joy.

John 2 opens with a far greater act of quiet mercy. At a wedding in Cana, Jesus' first miracle wasn't simply spectacular—it was compassionate. He turned water into wine, saving a family from public embarrassment and revealing the generous heart of God. The story overflows with symbolism: transformation, abundance, and new covenant joy. But the chapter doesn't end in celebration; it ends in confrontation. When Jesus entered the temple, he overturned tables and exposed corruption, showing that his mission was not only to fill but also to cleanse.

In this lesson, we'll see both sides of Christ's glory—the gentleness that sustains joy and the zeal that defends holiness. The same Savior who fills empty jars also purifies his Father's house. Together, these two scenes remind us that true faith rejoices in grace and submits to truth.

EXAMINATION

The Setting: A wedding in Cana (2:1-2)

If you want to understand Jesus, you could do worse than start with a wedding. John doesn't begin Jesus' public ministry with thunder or spectacle but with celebration. The first sign of the Messiah's glory appeared not in a temple or courtroom but at a family gathering in a small Galilean village. It was the third day after Jesus' calling of Nathanael, and everyone was still buzzing about this rabbi from Nazareth who might just be the One.

Jesus, his disciples, and his mother were invited to the feast. The presence of all three groups—family, followers, and friends—suggested a close connection to the hosts. Weddings in the ancient world were weeklong events with the entire community attending. Hospitality was a sacred duty, and running out of food or drink would bring lifelong shame.

The setting mattered. Before Jesus ever preached a sermon, he attended a party. That tells us something about God's heart. He is not aloof or allergic to human joy. The God who invented laughter, music, and marriage didn't hover on the edges of celebration—he stepped right into it. Jesus' first miracle wasn't raising the dead or silencing a storm; it was keeping a wedding reception from falling apart. The eternal Word who made the universe was now making sure the party didn't end too soon.

The shortage and the sign (2:3-11)

Disaster struck midway through the festivities: "They have no wine." Mary, ever attentive, noticed before most others. The statement carried both concern and urgency. In that culture, the groom's family bore responsibility for the feast's provisions. Running out of wine wasn't a minor inconvenience—it was a public embarrassment.

Mary turned to Jesus and simply stated the problem. She didn't tell him what to do; she just laid the need before him. That's prayer at its purest—no instructions, just trust. Jesus' reply, though, startles modern ears: "Woman, what does this have to do with me? My hour has not yet come." The term "woman" sounds cold in English, but in Greek it was respectful, similar to "ma'am." Still, the tone marked a shift in their relationship. Jesus' mission would no longer operate on family ties or maternal prompting but on divine timing.

Yet Mary's response revealed faith that understood more than words could express. She turned to the servants and said, "Do whatever he tells you." That line has preached a thousand sermons for good reason—it's the essence of discipleship. When you don't understand God's timing, obey his instruction.

Nearby stood six stone water jars, each holding twenty or thirty gallons, used for Jewish purification rites. Jesus told the servants to fill them "to the brim." There was no magic formula, no incantation, no flair—just quiet obedience. Then he told them to draw some out and take it to the master of the feast. Somewhere between the filling and the tasting, the ordinary became extraordinary. The water blushed into wine.

When the master of the feast tasted it, he was astonished. Not only had the wine returned—it had improved. "Everyone serves the good wine first," he said, "but you have kept the good wine until now." In the kingdom of God, the best is never behind us but always ahead. The new covenant Jesus inaugurated is superior to the old, just as this wine surpassed the first. The sign wasn't about fermentation—it was about fulfillment.

Notice also who witnessed the miracle: not the crowd, not the emcee, but the servants who obeyed. They filled, they drew, and they knew. God often lets the backstage workers see his power first.

The first glimpse of glory (2:11–12)

John calls this miracle the first of Jesus' "signs," not "wonders." A sign points beyond itself—it's not the destination but the direction. This one pointed to Jesus' identity as the life-giving Messiah. John concludes, "He manifested his glory, and his disciples believed in him." The miracle wasn't loud or public, but it quietly deepened faith in those already following him.

Jesus' glory in this moment was not the blinding radiance of Sinai but the warm glow of grace. The transformation of water into wine symbolized the transformation he came to bring—old becoming new, empty becoming full, shame replaced with joy. John's Gospel often pairs physical acts with spiritual meaning, and here we see the gospel in miniature: Jesus took what was common and made it glorious.

After the feast, Jesus, his mother, his brothers, and his disciples went down to Capernaum for a few days. It was the calm before the storm, a brief pause between celebration and confrontation. For now, the glory of God had appeared in laughter, not lightning—in abundance, not anger. But that was about to change.

The cleansing of the temple (2:13-22)

Passover approached, and Jesus went up to Jerusalem. The mood shifted from joy to judgment. In the temple courts, he found merchants selling oxen, sheep, and doves, and moneychangers seated at their tables. What began as a service for pilgrims had devolved into a religious flea market. Worship had been reduced to commerce, and reverence had given way to racket.

Jesus didn't quietly file a complaint with temple management. He made a whip of cords, drove out the animals, scattered the coins, and overturned the tables. It was a startling scene: the Prince of Peace swinging a whip in holy anger. Yet his fury wasn't uncontrolled—it was righteous zeal. "Take these things away; do not make my Father's house a house of trade."

The disciples remembered that it was written, "Zeal for your house will consume me." That line from Psalm 69 foretold a Messiah whose passion for God's holiness would cost him everything. The cleansing of the temple wasn't an outburst; it was a prophecy enacted. The One who turned water into wine now turned over tables—both acts revealing his authority to transform what had become corrupted.

The Jewish leaders demanded a sign to justify his actions. Jesus replied enigmatically, "Destroy this temple, and in three days I will raise it up." They scoffed—"It has taken forty-six years to build this temple, and will you raise it up in three days?" But John explains, "He was speaking about the temple of his body." Long before his crucifixion, Jesus pointed to his death and resurrection as the ultimate sign of divine authority.

When he rose from the dead, the disciples remembered this saying and believed the Scripture and the word Jesus had spoken. What they could not grasp in the moment became clear in the light of resurrection. Faith often works that way—we understand backward, even as we trust forward.

The misunderstood Messiah (2:23–25)

John closes the chapter with a sobering note: "Many believed in his name when they saw the signs that he was doing. But Jesus did not entrust himself to them, because he knew all people." Not all belief is saving belief. Some were fascinated by miracles but untouched by repentance. They wanted signs, not a Savior; spectacle, not surrender.

Jesus' insight into human nature was perfect. He didn't need anyone to tell him what was in a man, because he already knew. The same One who turned water into wine could read hearts like open books. His knowledge wasn't cynical but truthful—he understood our fragility and our fickleness.

This passage sets the tone for everything that follows. The One who came to bring joy also demands holiness. He filled empty jars and emptied corrupt temples. He revealed his glory in compassion and in confrontation. The same Jesus who gladdened a wedding feast also guards the sanctity of worship.

The contrast between Cana and the temple forms a powerful lesson: the glory of Jesus cannot be domesticated. He was gentle enough to save a celebration and fierce enough to cleanse a sanctuary. His mission was never to make people comfortable in their traditions but to call them into new life. At Cana, he revealed the heart of grace; in Jerusalem, the heart of truth. Both belonged to him, full and inseparable.

APPLICATION

1. Bring him your empty jars

When Mary said, "They have no wine," she didn't try to hide the shortage—she brought it to Jesus. Every Christian eventually faces an empty jar moment: joy running low, hope evaporating, faith stretched thin. The miracle began when someone admitted the lack. Jesus still delights to fill what we bring him, but he never fills what we pretend is already full. Discipleship starts with honesty. The servants obeyed simple instructions—fill, draw, carry—and found that obedience opens the door to transformation. When the jars are empty, don't despair; that's where grace begins to pour.

2. Expect his best to come last

The master of the feast marveled that the bridegroom had saved the best wine for last. That's how God works. The world offers its thrills early and leaves hangovers behind. Jesus saves his richest joys for those who wait. The miracle at Cana whispered of eternity—the ultimate wedding feast when heaven's celebration never runs dry. For now, believers taste grace in sips and glimpses, but one day, we'll drink deeply from the cup of joy that never ends. Faith means trusting that Christ's finest work is still ahead, even when circumstances taste bitter now.

3. Let him turn over your tables

The same Jesus who replenished joy also disrupted complacency. His cleansing of the temple reminds us that worship can lose its way. Sometimes the Lord must overturn our tables—comforts, habits, or attitudes that clutter his house. When Christ confronts our corruption, it isn't cruelty; it's mercy in motion. A faith that never gets challenged never gets purified. The Savior who filled the jars in Cana also cleared the courts in Jerusalem, proving that real devotion rejoices in both grace and truth. If he's overturning something in your life, it's because he's making room for something better.

4. Believe beyond the signs

Many in Jerusalem "believed" because of the miracles, but Jesus didn't trust their shallow faith. It's possible to be impressed by Jesus without being transformed by him. Mature faith rests not on spectacle but on the Savior himself. Signs are invitations, not destinations. The water-to-wine miracle pointed to something greater—the cross, where his blood would become the cup of the new covenant. The question isn't "What can Jesus do *for* me?" but "Who is Jesus *to* me?" Real faith doesn't end with amazement; it begins with allegiance.

CONCLUSION

In Cana, Jesus revealed his glory through quiet transformation; in the temple, he revealed it through righteous confrontation. Together, these scenes show the full heart of the Messiah—grace that restores and truth that refines. His power was not for spectacle but for renewal, turning water into wine and worship into purity.

Next, in John 3, the focus shifts from public signs to a private conversation. Under the cover of night, a Pharisee named Nicodemus will learn that real transformation happens not in stone jars or temple courts but in the human heart—through a new birth from above.

REFLECTION

1. What does Jesus' presence at a wedding reveal about God's view of joy and celebration?

2. How does Mary's statement, "Do whatever he tells you," challenge your own obedience to Christ?

3. In what ways do you identify with the "empty jars" at Cana?

4. How do the contrasting scenes at Cana and the temple reveal different sides of Jesus' glory?

5. What "tables" might Jesus need to overturn in your life or worship?

6. Why is it dangerous to base faith only on visible signs or miracles?

DISCUSSION

1. What lessons about prayer can we learn from Mary's quiet confidence at Cana?

2. How does Jesus' first miracle foreshadow his greater work on the cross?

3. Why do you think John paired the joyful wedding with the forceful temple cleansing in one chapter?

4. What practical steps help us recognize when our worship has become self-serving rather than God-centered?

5. How can Christians model both the grace of Cana and the truth of the temple in everyday life?

6. How does this chapter prepare us to understand Jesus' growing public ministry in the chapters that follow?

4

BORN FROM ABOVE

JOHN 3

Objective: To understand that true life comes only through new birth by the Spirit and faith in Jesus.

INTRODUCTION

A preacher once asked a group of children, "What do you have to do to be born?" One little boy thought for a moment and answered, "Nothing. Somebody else does all the work." Every adult in the room smiled—and then fell silent. The boy had accidentally summarized the gospel better than most theologians.

John 3 tells the story of a man who needed that same lesson. Nicodemus came to Jesus with credentials, confidence, and curiosity, but he lacked the one thing that mattered: new life. He was moral but not reborn, religious but not redeemed. Jesus met him under the cover of night and spoke words that would echo through every generation—"You must be born again."

In this chapter, Jesus revealed that spiritual life doesn't come through effort, status, or ritual but through the work of the Spirit. The kingdom isn't inherited; it's entered through rebirth. Later, John the Baptist would echo this truth in his final testimony: true joy comes when Christ increases and self decreases.

This lesson invites us to leave behind self-sufficiency and receive the life only heaven can give. The new birth isn't about trying harder; it's about starting over—being born from above by the grace of God.

EXAMINATION

Nicodemus comes by night (3:1-2)

John 3 opens with a man stepping out of the shadows. His name was Nicodemus—a Pharisee, a ruler of the Jews, and the kind of person everyone in Jerusalem recognized. He was educated, moral, and deeply religious. In short, he was the kind of man people would have assumed didn't need saving. Yet here he came, under cover of darkness, looking for something he couldn't find in daylight.

He addressed Jesus respectfully: "Rabbi, we know that you are a teacher come from God, for no one can do these signs that you do unless God is with him." Nicodemus came with compliments; Jesus answered with confrontation. The rabbi from Nazareth didn't thank him for the kind words or ask for an endorsement from the Sanhedrin. Instead, Jesus cut straight to the heart of the matter: "Truly, truly, I say to you, unless one is born again, he cannot see the kingdom of God."

The Greek phrase could also be translated "born from above." Both meanings fit perfectly. To see or enter the kingdom, a person must experience a birth that comes not from human effort but divine intervention. Nicodemus, master of law and lineage, now faced a truth no pedigree could solve: heaven doesn't recognize résumés—only rebirth.

Born of water and Spirit (3:3-8)

Nicodemus, to his credit, didn't scoff. But he also didn't understand. "How can a man be born when he is old? Can he enter a second time into his mother's womb?" You can almost hear the confusion—and maybe the nervous laugh. He took Jesus' words literally when Jesus was speaking spiritually. The teacher of Israel had met the Teacher from heaven, and he was out of his depth.

Jesus explained further: "Unless one is born of water and the Spirit, he cannot enter the kingdom of God." Scholars have argued for centuries over what "water" means. In the context of John's Gospel, it likely points to baptism, to cleansing, and to renewal—the promise of Ezekiel 36:25-27, where God said he would sprinkle clean water and give a new heart by his Spirit. In other words, Jesus was saying that entry into God's kingdom required inner transformation, not outward conformity.

"Flesh gives birth to flesh, and Spirit gives birth to spirit." Human effort produces human results; only the Spirit produces spiritual life. Religion can reform a person; regeneration transforms them. Jesus then used a vivid analogy: "The wind blows where it wishes, and you hear its sound, but you do not know where it comes from or where it goes." Like the wind, the Spirit is invisible but undeniably real. You can't see his arrival, but you can't miss his effects. Nicodemus, who had likely spent years studying God, was now realizing how little he truly understood him.

Earthly questions and heavenly answers (3:9-15)

"How can these things be?" Nicodemus asked. His tone was more bewildered than defiant. Jesus replied with gentle rebuke: "Are you the teacher of Israel and yet you do not understand these things?" The problem wasn't intelligence but insight. Nicodemus knew the Scriptures but had missed their heartbeat.

Jesus continued, contrasting earthly ignorance with heavenly authority. "We speak of what we know, and bear witness to what we have seen, but you do not receive our testimony." The plural "we" probably included both Jesus and John the Baptist—the witnesses heaven had already sent. If Nicodemus couldn't grasp the basic truths about spiritual birth, how could he handle heavenly mysteries?

Then Jesus made a surprising reference to the Old Testament: "As Moses lifted up the serpent in the wilderness, so must the Son of Man be lifted up, that whoever believes in him may have eternal life." The story comes from Numbers 21, when Israel complained in the wilderness and God sent venomous snakes as judgment. The people repented, and God instructed Moses to make a bronze serpent on a pole. Whoever looked at it lived. Jesus took that familiar image and turned it into prophecy. He would be lifted up—on the cross—so that everyone who looked to him in faith would live.

Nicodemus wanted a theological formula; Jesus offered a crucified Savior. The cure for the poison of sin wouldn't come from law-keeping or moral polish but from looking to the One raised up for all.

God's love for the world (3:16-21)

John's commentary reaches its most famous crescendo in verse 16, a verse so familiar that its wonder is often lost in repetition: "For God so loved the world that he gave his only Son, that whoever believes in him should not perish but have eternal life."

The word "so" doesn't measure quantity but manner—God loved the world this way: by giving his Son. The "world" (Greek *kosmos*) doesn't mean humanity at its best but humanity in rebellion. The same world that has rejected light still receives love. God's initiative began not with our merit but with his mercy.

Jesus didn't come to condemn the world but to save it. Condemnation was already the default setting of fallen humanity; salvation required intervention. Those who believe in the Son step into light and life; those who refuse remain in darkness by choice.

John uses light imagery again to describe human response. "Light has come into the world, and people loved the darkness rather than the light because their works were evil." Sin thrives in secrecy. The tragedy isn't ignorance—it's preference. Humanity doesn't merely stumble in the dark; it hides there. But those who come to the light prove that their deeds are "carried out in God." The gospel exposes and redeems at the same time.

In Nicodemus, the reader sees both the struggle and the hope. The man who came by night eventually defended Jesus before the Sanhedrin (7:50-52) and helped bury him after the crucifixion (19:39). The light that first startled him eventually saved him.

John the Baptist's final testimony (3:22-36)

The narrative shifts from Jerusalem back to the countryside, where Jesus and his disciples were baptizing. John the Baptist was still active nearby, and some of his followers grew concerned: "Rabbi, he who was with you across the Jordan, to whom you bore witness—look, he is baptizing, and all are going to him [Ministry envy is as old as ministry itself.]."

John answered with the humility of a man who knew his role. "A person cannot receive even one thing unless it is given him from heaven." His joy wasn't diminished by Jesus' growing fame—it was fulfilled by it. He compared himself to the best man at a wedding: "The friend of the bridegroom rejoices greatly at the bridegroom's voice." Then came his most famous line: "He must increase, but I must decrease." Those seven words summarize the proper posture of every servant of Christ.

John also delivered his final theological testimony. Jesus, the One from heaven, speaks the words of God because he gives the Spirit without measure. The Father loves the Son and has placed all things in his hands. The conclusion was clear and uncompromising: "Whoever believes in the Son has eternal life; whoever does not obey the Son shall not see life, but the wrath of God remains on him."

The chapter that began with a respected religious leader sneaking through shadows ends with a wilderness prophet joyfully stepping aside. Nicodemus came in darkness seeking understanding; John stood in daylight proclaiming surrender. Both met the same truth—life is found only in the Son.

APPLICATION

1. Religion isn't rebirth

Nicodemus proved that sincerity and scholarship can't substitute for new birth. He knew Scripture, obeyed rules, and sat in positions of power—but he still needed transformation. Many people today live like spiritual accountants, assuming their good deeds balance out the bad. Jesus shattered that illusion. Rebirth isn't earned; it's received. The Spirit gives what flesh never can. Our task isn't to polish the old life but to surrender to the new one. The gospel doesn't make people nicer—it makes them new.

2. Let the Spirit blow where he wills

Jesus compared the Spirit's work to the wind—unseen, uncontrollable, and undeniable. That's a humbling truth for anyone who prefers predictability. The Spirit refuses to stay within our formulas or schedules. He moves through unlikely people, unexpected moments, and undeserved grace. Discipleship means cooperating with that divine unpredictability. We can't manufacture spiritual life in others, but we can remove obstacles, obey promptly, and remain receptive. Like Nicodemus, we often feel the wind before we understand its source. The call is to trust the movement, not to map it.

3. Look and live

When Jesus referenced Moses' bronze serpent, he described salvation in the simplest terms: look and live. The Israelites weren't cured by effort or ritual but by trust—by looking up. That pattern still holds. The cross stands as God's great invitation for all who have been bitten by sin's venom. Faith isn't a leap into darkness but a gaze into light. We don't fix ourselves; we fix our eyes on the Son lifted up. Salvation isn't about achieving but receiving, not climbing but clinging.

4. He must increase, we must decrease

John the Baptist's final words form the motto of every mature Christian. Real joy doesn't come from spotlight or status but from seeing Jesus exalted. When his presence grows in our lives, our ego naturally shrinks. "He must increase" isn't a slogan for preachers—it's a prayer for every Christian. Whether in success or obscurity, our purpose is the same: to make much of Christ. If we measure our lives by applause, we'll live anxiously; if we measure them by faithfulness, we'll live free.

CONCLUSION

Nicodemus came to Jesus in the shadows, searching for answers, and left with an invitation—to be born from above. Jesus revealed that eternal life begins not with effort but with rebirth, not with religion but with the Spirit. God's love reaches down, offering light to those trapped in darkness, and John the Baptist reminds us that true joy comes when Christ increases and self decreases.

In the next lesson, that same message moves to a Samaritan well. Jesus will meet a woman with a very different story but the same need—a thirsty heart longing for living water. The teacher and the outcast both discover the same truth: only Jesus can make life new.

REFLECTION

1. Why do you think Nicodemus, a respected teacher, sought out Jesus under the cover of night?

2. What does it mean to be "born from above," and how have you experienced that transformation?

3. How does Jesus' comparison of the Spirit to the wind help you understand the Spirit's work?

4. What stands out to you about God's love in John 3:16 when you read it slowly and personally?

5. What does John the Baptist's statement, "He must increase, but I must decrease," reveal about true humility?

6. How has your understanding of faith changed as you've learned to "look and live"?

DISCUSSION

1. What does Nicodemus's encounter teach us about the limits of religion and the necessity of rebirth?

2. How can the church balance biblical or theological knowledge with dependence on the Spirit's unpredictable work?

3. Why is the image of the bronze serpent such a powerful picture of salvation through Christ?

4. How does John 3:16 correct both pride and despair in our understanding of God's grace?

5. What practical steps can help believers cultivate the humility expressed in "He must increase, I must decrease"?

6. How does John 3 prepare us for Jesus' next encounter—with the Samaritan woman in John 4?

5

LIVING WATER
JOHN 4

Objective: To understand that Jesus alone gives living water—satisfying the soul, transforming worship, and calling all to faith.

INTRODUCTION

In 1936, the Hoover Dam began sending water through the parched valleys of the American Southwest. For centuries, that land had known only drought and dust. Suddenly, rivers ran where the ground had cracked, and entire towns came to life. Engineers didn't change the desert—they just brought water to it.

That's a picture of what Jesus did for one woman in John 4. Her soul was a desert—dry from disappointment, cracked by shame, and tired from carrying the same old bucket to the same old well. Then she met the One who offered "living water," a spring that never runs out. The conversation began with thirst and ended with worship, spreading revival through a town everyone else had written off.

John 4 shows that no one is too far gone and no place too far out for grace to reach. The Savior who knew everything about her still offered her everything she needed. He broke barriers, exposed wounds, and poured life where there had only been drought. Later in the chapter, he healed a dying boy from miles away, proving that his word carries power across every distance.

EXAMINATION

The journey through Samaria (4:1–6)

John 4 opens with an unexpected travel itinerary. When Jesus learned that the Pharisees were tracking his growing ministry, he left Judea and headed north toward Galilee. But instead of taking the long detour around Samaria—as most Jews did—he "had to" pass through it. That little phrase isn't about geography; it is about grace. The route was necessary not because of terrain but because of mission.

Samaria was the land that respectable Jews avoided. Centuries earlier, when the Assyrians conquered the northern kingdom (722 BC), they had resettled foreigners there who intermarried with the remaining Israelites, blending religion and ethnicity into a hybrid faith. To the Jews of Jesus' day, Samaritans were half-breeds and heretics. Yet Jesus walked straight into their territory, not to debate theology but to seek a thirsty soul.

We find him weary from the journey, sitting beside Jacob's well around noon—the hottest hour of the day. The Son of God, who created oceans and rivers, sat tired and thirsty beside a well he once spoke into existence. It was a picture of divine humility: the Living Water waiting for a drink.

The conversation at the well (4:7–15)

A woman came alone to draw water, a detail that speaks volumes. Most women gathered water in the cool of the morning, chatting together as they worked. Her solitary trip under the noonday sun hints at social shame. Jesus broke both custom and expectation by speaking first: "Give me a drink." Jewish rabbis didn't converse with women in public—certainly not with Samaritans. His simple request shattered centuries of prejudice in one sentence.

The woman's response was laced with skepticism: "How is it that you, a Jew, ask for a drink from me, a woman of Samaria?" Jesus turned the conversation from water in a bucket to water for the soul. "If you knew the gift of God, and who it is that is saying to you, 'Give me a drink,' you would have asked him, and he would have given you living water."

She misunderstood, of course. Her thoughts stayed on the physical plane. "Sir, you have nothing to draw water with, and the well is deep." To her, Jesus sounded like a strange man without a rope promising better plumbing. But Jesus pressed further. "Everyone who drinks of this water will be thirsty again, but whoever drinks of the water that I will give him will never be thirsty forever."

This wasn't a sales pitch—it was salvation language. The living water represented the life of the Spirit, satisfying the deepest thirst of the human heart. Religion could draw from Jacob's well, but only Jesus could quench the soul. The woman's curiosity turned to desire: "Sir, give me this water." She didn't understand it fully, but she knew she wanted it. That's often how faith begins—half-understood longing stirred by grace.

Exposing the heart (4:16–26)

Before she could drink living water, Jesus had to expose the leak in her soul. "Go, call your husband, and come here." The request sounds ordinary, but it pierced like a scalpel. "I have no husband," she answered. Jesus replied gently but truthfully, "You are right in saying, 'I have no husband'; for you have had five husbands, and the one you now have is not your husband."

There was no cruelty in his tone, only clarity. Jesus revealed truth not to condemn her but to confront the false wells she had dug in pursuit of satisfaction—relationships, reputation, maybe even religion. Sin had parched her soul; now grace offered her a drink.

The woman quickly changed the subject: "Sir, I perceive that you are a prophet. Our fathers worshiped on this mountain, but you say that in Jerusalem is the place where people ought to worship." It's a classic human move—divert from conviction by debating doctrine. Jesus didn't dismiss her question but redirected it: "The hour is coming when neither on this mountain nor in Jerusalem will you worship the Father." True worship, he explained, wasn't about geography but sincerity: "God is spirit, and those who worship him must worship in spirit and truth."

For centuries, worship had been tied to places, rituals, and boundaries. Jesus declared that the Father sought worshipers, not tourists. True worship would no longer depend on temples of stone but on hearts made alive by the Spirit. The woman, still reaching for clarity, said, "I know that Messiah is coming… When he comes, he will tell us all things." Jesus answered, "I who speak to you am he." It is the first time in John's Gospel that Jesus explicitly reveals his messiahship—and he chose to do it for a Samaritan woman with a messy past.

The witness of the woman (4:27–42)

At that moment, the disciples returned and were visibly uncomfortable. They didn't dare question Jesus aloud, but their faces probably said enough. The woman, meanwhile, left her water jar—the very reason she'd come—and hurried back to town. When you've found living water, you forget your bucket.

Her message was simple and raw: "Come, see a man who told me all that I ever did. Can this be the Christ?" She didn't preach a sermon; she shared an encounter. The villagers' curiosity was piqued, and they came to see for themselves. Many believed because of her testimony; many more believed after hearing Jesus firsthand. The outcast became an evangelist, and the despised town of Sychar became the first Samaritan revival.

Jesus used the moment to teach his disciples a lesson about mission. While they urged him to eat, he said, "My food is to do the will of him who sent me and to accomplish his work." He spoke of fields ripe for harvest, inviting his followers to join in reaping souls they hadn't sown. The Samaritan woman had done what the disciples hadn't yet learned to do—she'd shared the gospel across cultural boundaries. The men who thought they were the workers turned out to be the spectators.

John notes that Jesus stayed two days with the Samaritans—unthinkable for a Jewish rabbi. The townspeople declared, "We know that this is indeed the Savior of the world." That title was no small confession. The gospel had just crossed its first cultural border, and the outcasts were among the first to recognize the King.

The healing of the official's son (4:43–54)

After his time in Samaria, Jesus returned to Galilee, where prophets were famously unwelcome in their own country. Yet he was received by those who had seen his signs in Jerusalem. Among them came a royal official from Capernaum whose son was near death. Desperation has a way of leveling titles; when your child is dying, you stop worrying about dignity. The man begged Jesus to come and heal him.

Jesus' reply sounded abrupt: "Unless you see signs and wonders, you will not believe." He wasn't scolding the father alone but the miracle-hungry mentality of the crowd. Yet the man persisted, "Sir, come down before my child dies." Faith often begins in desperation, but Jesus wanted to move this man from sight to trust. He said simply, "Go; your son will live."

The man believed the word Jesus spoke and started home. That's one of the quietest and greatest miracles in John's Gospel—a man walked home with nothing but a promise. As he neared Capernaum, servants met him with good news: his son was alive. When he asked the hour of recovery, they said, "Yesterday at the seventh hour the fever left him." It was the exact moment Jesus had spoken.

John concludes: "He himself believed, and all his household." The chapter that started with a weary Savior at a well concludes with a powerful Savior at a distance. Jesus didn't need to touch, travel, or even see the boy. His word was enough. The woman at the well believed because he knew everything she'd done; the official believed because he said only one thing: "Your son will live." Faith takes many shapes, but it always rests on the same foundation—his word.

APPLICATION

1. Break barriers to reach people

Jesus didn't have to pass through Samaria, but he chose to. The gospel moves most powerfully when we cross lines others avoid—cultural, racial, social, or personal. He met a woman everyone else avoided and treated her with dignity and truth. Discipleship means going where polite religion refuses to go. If we're too careful to stay comfortable, we'll miss the wells where grace is waiting. Sometimes the shortest route to a person's heart is through the road everyone else walks around.

2. Stop drinking from empty wells

The woman at the well kept returning to the same source that never satisfied, just as she kept seeking fulfillment in relationships that always ran dry. Jesus exposed her thirst not to shame her but to save her. Every generation still digs its own wells—success, romance, money, approval—but none can quench the soul. Living water isn't found in what we earn or control; it's found in who we trust. The first step toward healing is admitting that the bucket's empty. Only when we let go of false wells can we drink deeply of grace.

3. Worship in spirit and truth

The woman tried to shift the conversation to religious geography—"this mountain or that one?" Jesus answered with liberation: true worship isn't confined to a place but shaped by the heart. Spirit and truth go together—zeal without truth burns out, and truth without spirit dries up. Worship happens wherever surrendered hearts adore the Father through the Son. Whether in a church building, a hospital room, or a kitchen sink, the question isn't where we worship but how. If worship feels lifeless, it may be time to trade performance for presence.

4. Believe the Word, even before you see

The royal official's story reminds us that mature faith walks on promises, not proofs. Jesus sent him home with nothing but a word—"Your son will live"—and the man believed. That's faith in its purest form: trusting what Jesus says even before we see what he does. Every Christian will face moments when God's word seems all we have. But that word is enough. The same voice that turned water into wine and calmed the storm still speaks life into our fears. Faith walks home on the strength of his sentence.

CONCLUSION

At a lonely well, Jesus revealed that only he can satisfy the thirsts that drain the soul. The Samaritan woman discovered what every seeker must—that true life begins when we stop hiding and start drinking from the living water he offers. Her testimony transformed a town, and a royal official's faith showed that his word still gives life, even from a distance. The outcast and the nobleman both found what Nicodemus sought: new life from above.

In the next chapter, Jesus' compassion continues at a pool in Jerusalem, where a man's long sickness meets the power of his command. The One who offered living water will speak healing into weakness and confront unbelief with authority.

REFLECTION

1. What does Jesus' choice to travel through Samaria reveal about his heart for the overlooked?

2. Which "empty wells" have you seen people turn to for meaning and satisfaction?

3. How does Jesus' knowledge of the Samaritan woman's past deepen your trust in his compassion?

4. What does it mean to you personally to worship "in spirit and truth"?

5. How does the royal official's response challenge the way you practice faith in uncertainty?

6. In what area of your life do you most need to believe his word before you see results?

DISCUSSION

1. Why was Jesus' conversation with the Samaritan woman so shocking in its cultural context?

2. How can Christians today follow Jesus' example in breaking social or religious barriers for the gospel?

3. What are some modern "false wells" the church must help people stop drinking from?

4. How does the woman's transformation model effective evangelism for ordinary believers?

5. What can the healing of the official's son teach us about trusting God's timing and authority?

6. How does John 4 prepare us for Jesus' later statement, "I am the bread of life," in John 6?

6

AUTHORITY OF THE SON
JOHN 5

Objective: To recognize Jesus' divine authority to give life, confront unbelief, and call the powerless to rise and walk.

INTRODUCTION

In 1968, a young marathon runner from Tanzania fell and dislocated his knee during the Mexico City Olympics. Hours after the race ended, when the stadium was nearly empty, he limped across the finish line. Asked why he didn't quit, he replied, "My country didn't send me 5,000 miles to start the race. They sent me to finish it." His perseverance stirred hearts around the world.

In John 5, Jesus meets a man who had been lying by a pool for thirty-eight years. Then the Son of God came to him and said, "Rise, take up your bed, and walk." One command from Jesus accomplished what decades of effort never could.

This chapter reveals Jesus' authority to restore the powerless and to confront the proud. The miracle at Bethesda exposed both the compassion of the Savior and the blindness of the religious leaders. When challenged, Jesus boldly declared his unity with the Father and his right to give life and execute judgment. The one who healed the helpless man was no ordinary teacher—he was the Lord of life himself.

In this lesson, we'll see that grace meets us where we're stuck, and the Word of Christ still raises us to walk.

EXAMINATION

The Setting: The pool of Bethesda (5:1-5)

John 5 opens with Jesus returning to Jerusalem for a Jewish feast. While the exact festival isn't named, the focus quickly turns away from celebration to suffering. Near the Sheep Gate, where lambs once entered for sacrifice, lay a pool called Bethesda—"house of mercy." The name was ironic. Mercy seemed scarce there.

Around the pool gathered a crowd of broken bodies and weary souls. The place was known for a legend that, when the water stirred, the first person to enter would be healed. It was the ancient equivalent of a spiritual lottery—one winner, countless losers. John introduces one man who had been an invalid for thirty-eight years. That's nearly four decades of waiting, watching others move ahead while he stayed stuck.

The pool was full of desperation but empty of compassion. Everyone there was too busy hoping for their own miracle to notice anyone else's misery. And into that scene of futility stepped Jesus. He didn't come for the pomp or applause; he came for one man who couldn't come to him.

"Do you want to be healed?" (5:6-9)

When Jesus saw the man lying there, he knew his condition had lasted a long time. Then came one of the most disarming questions in Scripture: "Do you want to be healed?" It almost sounds insulting—who wouldn't? But Jesus' question pierced deeper than physical illness. Some wounds become identities; some conditions become excuses.

The man's response revealed more resignation than faith: "Sir, I have no one to put me into the pool when the water is stirred up, and while I am going another steps down before me." His focus was still on the water, not the Word standing before him. For thirty-eight years, he'd been waiting for someone to help him into the pool; now the healer was offering to raise him out of it.

Jesus said to him, "Get up, take up your bed, and walk." The command required obedience before evidence. There was no hand-holding, no ritual, no delay—just the authority of divine speech. At once, the man was healed; he picked up his mat and walked.

It's worth noting that Jesus didn't heal everyone at the pool. His mercy was particular but purposeful, a sign meant to reveal his identity as the life-giver. Grace doesn't follow formulas. It moves freely, personally, and powerfully.

Sabbath controversy (5:10–16)

The healing, however, caused an uproar. John points out a detail that set off the conflict: "Now that day was the Sabbath." The religious leaders saw a man carrying his mat and immediately reached for their rulebooks. Instead of rejoicing over his recovery, they reprimanded him for violating Sabbath law. Legalism has a way of missing miracles.

When they asked why he was carrying his mat, the man explained, "The man who healed me said to me, 'Take up your bed, and walk.'" The leaders didn't celebrate the healer; they interrogated the healed. "Who is the man who said to you, 'Take up your bed and walk'?" At this point, the man didn't even know Jesus' name. The grace that restored him hadn't yet led to recognition.

Later, Jesus found him in the temple—a beautiful detail. The man who once couldn't enter the temple now stood in it, restored. Jesus said to him, "See, you are well! Sin no more, that nothing worse may happen to you." Not every sickness is caused by sin, but all sin leads to something worse than sickness—spiritual death. The healing pointed beyond health to holiness.

When the man reported that it was Jesus who had healed him, the Jewish leaders' hostility intensified. John writes, "This was why the Jews were persecuting Jesus, because he was doing these things on the Sabbath." Grace had collided with guardians of tradition. The One who came to give rest was accused of breaking it.

The authority of the Son (5:17–30)

Jesus responded not with apology but with revelation: "My Father is working until now, and I am working." That single sentence ignited a theological explosion. The Jews understood exactly what he meant. By calling God his own Father, Jesus was claiming equality with God. The Sabbath controversy escalated into a claim of divine identity.

Jesus explained that his work was not independent of the Father's but perfectly aligned with it: "The Son can do nothing of his own accord, but only what he sees the Father doing." Far from undermining God's authority, his actions expressed it. The Father and Son were not competitors but co-workers in creation and redemption.

He went further, describing the Father's love in active terms: "For the Father loves the Son and shows him all that he himself is doing." Their unity wasn't mechanical but relational—an eternal fellowship of love that overflowed into a universal rescue mission.

Then came a breathtaking declaration: "As the Father raises the dead and gives them life, so also the Son gives life to whom he will." Only God can give life or execute judgment, yet Jesus claimed both prerogatives. He added, "The Father judges no one, but has given all judgment to the Son." In other words, the authority of life and judgment rested in his hands.

Jesus called for a response: "Whoever does not honor the Son does not honor the Father who sent him." The claim was staggering. To reject Jesus was to reject God. He concluded with one of the Gospel's most comforting promises: "Truly, truly, I say to you, whoever hears my word and believes him who sent me has eternal life. He does not come into judgment but has passed from death to life." Salvation isn't a future possibility; it is a present reality for all who believe.

Jesus described two kinds of resurrection: one spiritual and one physical. The first happens now—when the spiritually dead hear his voice and live. The second will happen at the end of time—when all in their graves hear his voice and rise, some to life and others to judgment. The same voice that called Lazarus out of the tomb will one day call the world to account.

Witnesses to his identity (5:31–47)

Jewish law required two or three witnesses to confirm a testimony. Jesus, anticipating that principle, listed several witnesses to his identity. First, there was John the Baptist, who testified to the light. Then there were Jesus' works—the miracles themselves, signs that validated his divine commission. Next was the Father, whose voice and mission affirmed the Son. And finally, there were the Scriptures, which pointed to him all along.

"You search the Scriptures because you think that in them you have eternal life," Jesus said, "and it is they that bear witness about me, yet you refuse to come to me that you may have life." The tragedy of religion without relationship is knowing the text but missing the Author.

Jesus exposed the root problem: they sought human glory instead of God's. "I do not receive glory from people," he said. "How can you believe, when you receive glory from one another and do not seek the glory that comes from the only God?" Pride kept them blind. The very law they claimed to defend would one day accuse them. "If you believed Moses," Jesus said, "you would believe me; for he wrote of me."

John 5 closes not with healing but with hostility. Yet even in rejection, Jesus revealed his identity. He was not a Sabbath breaker but the Sabbath maker—the Lord who gives rest, life, and judgment. The man at the pool rose and walked because the Word of life spoke. Those who believe that same Word rise too—not just from sickbeds, but from sin and death itself.

APPLICATION

1. Grace finds us where we're stuck

The man at Bethesda didn't call for Jesus—Jesus came for him. That's grace in motion. He met the helpless, not the hopeful. After thirty-eight years, the man had stopped dreaming of change, but grace still walked through the crowd and called his name. Many of us have places in life that feel just as stuck: habits that won't break, fears that won't fade, prayers that feel unanswered. Jesus' question—"Do you want to be healed?"—still probes our will, not our worth. His power begins where our excuses end. When we've run out of strategies, his word still says, "Rise, take up your bed, and walk."

2. Beware the religion that misses God's work

The religious leaders saw a healed man carrying his mat and scolded him for breaking a rule. They prized regulations more than restoration. Legalism always protects systems over souls. Jesus' actions exposed their blindness—they could quote Moses but couldn't recognize the Messiah. Faith that measures holiness by rule-keeping will eventually miss the heart of God. The Sabbath wasn't designed to limit compassion but to celebrate the Creator who gives rest. The truest sign of faith isn't strictness but joy when grace shows up. When others rise and walk, we should celebrate, not calculate.

3. Honor the Son as you honor the Father

Jesus' bold claim of equality with God leaves no middle ground. We can't treat him as a wise teacher or moral reformer; he is either divine or deceptive. The Father gave him authority to give life and to judge—a staggering truth that demands reverence. To honor God rightly, we must honor his Son completely. That means more than confession; it means surrender. When Jesus acts, he doesn't act apart from the Father but as the full expression of his will. Every act of compassion, every word of truth, and every promise of life carries heaven's signature. Believing in Jesus isn't an alternative to worshiping God—it's the only way to do so.

4. Let Scripture lead you to the Savior

The Jewish leaders knew the Scriptures by heart but missed the heart of Scripture. Knowledge without submission becomes arrogance, not faith. It's possible to search the Bible and still stay thirsty if we never come to the One it reveals. Every page whispers Jesus' name. The law exposes our need; the prophets announce his coming; the Gospels unveil his glory. Bible study should always end in worship, not argument. Like the man at the pool, we meet healing in and through the Word of God. The goal of Bible knowledge isn't information—it's transformation by the One who still says, "Rise and walk."

CONCLUSION

At the Pool of Bethesda, Jesus showed that his power reaches those who can't reach for him. One command—"Rise and walk"—turned despair into movement and exposed a religion that prized rules more than redemption. When challenged, Jesus revealed his true identity: the Son who works in perfect unity with the Father, giving life and exercising judgment. The healer of one man proved to be the Lord of all.

In the next chapter, his authority will extend beyond one person to a multitude. On a hillside in Galilee, Jesus will feed five thousand hungry souls and teach that he himself is the Bread of Life—the only one who satisfies both body and spirit.

REFLECTION

1. What does Jesus' question, "Do you want to be healed?" reveal about human nature and faith?

2. How does the story of the man at Bethesda show God's grace toward those who feel forgotten?

3. What does this miracle teach you about obedience before understanding or evidence?

4. How does Jesus' claim of equality with the Father shape your view of his authority?

5. When have you been tempted to focus on religious rules instead of spiritual renewal?

6. How does studying Scripture draw you closer to Jesus personally rather than just intellectually?

DISCUSSION

1. Why did Jesus choose to heal only one man at the pool? What might that teach us about grace?

2. What modern examples show how religion can miss the miracles happening around it?

3. How can believers today "rise and walk" in response to Jesus' call?

4. What does Jesus' authority to give life and judge reveal about his relationship with the Father?

5. How can we ensure that our study of Scripture leads us to worship, not just knowledge?

6. How does this chapter prepare us for the deeper conflicts that arise in John 6 and beyond?

7

THE BREAD OF LIFE

JOHN 6

Objective: To understand that Jesus, the Bread of Life, alone satisfies our deepest hunger and sustains true faith.

INTRODUCTION

In 2010, when thirty-three miners were trapped underground in Chile, the world watched as rescuers drilled through two thousand feet of rock to reach them. For sixty-nine days, the miners survived on measured rations and sheer hope. When the first rescue capsule finally surfaced, the men emerged singing hymns and shouting, "We are alive!" They knew what every survivor learns—life depends on what sustains you.

John 6 tells of another kind of hunger and another kind of rescue. Crowds followed Jesus for bread and miracles, but he wanted to give them something greater—himself. On a hillside, he fed thousands; on the sea, he calmed fear; and in the synagogue, he declared, "I am the bread of life." Those words invited faith but divided followers. Some believed, but many walked away.

This chapter reminds us that Jesus doesn't merely provide bread—he is the bread. Real life begins not when we get what we want from him, but when we find all we need in him. The Christ who satisfies hunger also tests commitment. Every disciple must decide whether to follow the crowd or stay with the Savior who alone gives the words of eternal life.

EXAMINATION

The feeding of the five thousand (6:1-15)

John 6 opens with a scene of both need and opportunity. A large crowd followed Jesus because of the miracles they had seen, not yet realizing that the greatest sign was standing right in front of them. Jesus went up a mountain near the Sea of Galilee and looked out on thousands of people who had come hungry for healing—and now just plain hungry.

When Jesus turned to Philip and asked, "Where are we to buy bread, so that these people may eat?" John notes that he said this to test him. Jesus already knew what he was going to do, but Philip's math failed him. He calculated cost, not compassion: "Two hundred denarii [i.e., two hundred days' wages for a common laborer] worth of bread would not be enough for each of them to get a little." Andrew tried a different kind of logic—faith mixed with realism: "There is a boy here who has five barley loaves and two fish, but what are they for so many?"

Jesus had the crowd sit down—five thousand men, not counting women and children—and gave thanks. He distributed the bread and fish until everyone was full. When they gathered the leftovers, twelve baskets overflowed. The One who created grain from soil and fish from sea multiplied both from a child's lunch. Scarcity turns to abundance in the hands of the Creator.

The miracle stirred the crowd's excitement. They said, "This is indeed the Prophet who is to come into the world." But their enthusiasm quickly became political. They wanted to make him king by force—a bread king, not a cross-bearing Messiah. Knowing this, Jesus withdrew to the mountain alone. The One who could feed thousands refused to be crowned by their appetites.

Walking on the water (6:16-21)

That evening, the disciples set out across the lake toward Capernaum while Jesus remained behind. As night fell, the wind rose and the waters grew rough. After rowing three or four miles, they saw Jesus walking on the sea and approaching the boat. Fear gripped them until they heard his voice: "It is I; do not be afraid."

This wasn't a parlor trick to impress the disciples—it was a revelation of identity. The phrase "It is I" echoes God's own self-disclosure: I AM. The

One who fed the hungry now strode across the chaos of creation. The sea, symbol of disorder and danger, bowed beneath his feet.

John notes that as soon as they welcomed him into the boat, "immediately the boat was at the land to which they were going." The One who transcended distance also transcended danger. The miracle wasn't just about Jesus walking on water but about his presence transforming fear into arrival. The Christian life often feels like rowing against wind and wave; this story reminds us that the storm isn't the end when Christ is near.

The crowd's pursuit (6:22–29)

The next day, the crowd realized Jesus had crossed the lake and hurried after him. They weren't seeking truth—they were chasing another meal. "Rabbi, when did you come here?" they asked, but Jesus exposed their motives: "You are seeking me, not because you saw signs, but because you ate your fill of the loaves."

Then he offered a challenge: "Do not work for the food that perishes, but for the food that endures to eternal life." They wanted full stomachs; he offered full hearts. The crowd asked, "What must we do, to be doing the works of God?" Jesus answered simply, "This is the work of God, that you believe in him whom he has sent."

They wanted a task list; he offered himself. The bread they had eaten on the hillside could satisfy hunger for a few hours; the bread he offered would satisfy forever. Yet their thinking was still transactional—they wanted to earn what only grace could give.

The bread of life discourse (6:30–59)

The crowd demanded another sign, comparing Jesus to Moses: "Our fathers ate the manna in the wilderness." Jesus replied, "It was not Moses who gave you the bread from heaven, but my Father gives you the true bread from heaven." The manna in the wilderness sustained Israel temporarily; the true bread—Jesus himself—brings eternal life.

"I am the bread of life," he declared. "Whoever comes to me shall not hunger, and whoever believes in me shall never thirst." This is the first of John's seven "I Am" statements [Refernces?]. The crowd murmured—just like their ancestors who grumbled about manna in the desert. "Is not this Jesus, the son of Joseph?" they asked, unwilling to see beyond his humanity to his divinity.

Jesus continued: "No one can come to me unless the Father who sent me draws him." Grace always makes the first move. He promised resurrection to all who believe, declaring, "Everyone who looks on the Son and believes in him should have eternal life, and I will raise him up on the last day."

Then his words grew more startling: "The bread that I will give for the life of the world is my flesh." The Jews disputed among themselves, saying, "How can this man give us his flesh to eat?" Jesus pressed the point, not retreating from the metaphor: "Unless you eat the flesh of the Son of Man and drink his blood, you have no life in you."

He wasn't advocating cannibalism—he was describing communion. to eat his flesh and drink his blood meant to receive his life through faith, internalizing his sacrifice. The language was intentionally offensive to those who sought miracles without meaning. Jesus wanted followers, not fans.

He added, "Whoever feeds on my flesh and drinks my blood has eternal life, and I will raise him up on the last day." In saying this, Jesus connected the cross to sustenance—his death would become the nourishment of eternal life. Just as food sustains physical life, faith in the crucified Son sustains the soul.

The entire discourse reversed the crowd's logic. They wanted another handout; Jesus offered himself. They wanted to fill their bellies; he wanted to fill their beings. The only bread that truly satisfies is the One broken for us.

Many turn away (6:60–71)

The conversation that began with thousands ended with a handful. "This is a hard saying; who can listen to it?" many of his disciples said. They had followed him for the "show," not the surrender. When the cost of faith became clear, they walked away. Jesus didn't chase them with easier terms. He asked the Twelve, "Do you want to go away as well?"

Simon Peter answered with one of Scripture's most beautiful confessions: "Lord, to whom shall we go? You have the words of eternal life, and we have believed, and have come to know, that you are the Holy One of God."

Peter didn't claim to understand everything—only to know that Jesus alone had life. Real faith isn't built on perfect comprehension but on perfect trust in the One who never fails.

John notes that even among the Twelve was a traitor—Judas, who would later betray him. The chapter that began with abundance and applause ends with division and decision. Following Jesus means more than eating his bread; it means trusting his cross.

APPLICATION

1. Beware of following Jesus for the wrong reasons

The crowd followed Jesus because he filled their stomachs, not their souls. It's possible to admire his miracles without submitting to his lordship. Many still approach him as a means to an end—prosperity, comfort, healing, or relief—but discipleship means wanting him, not just his help. Jesus withdrew from the crowd that tried to crown him king because he refuses to rule on our terms. True faith seeks the Giver, not the gift. When we chase after temporary bread, we miss eternal life. Following Jesus begins when we stop asking, "What can he do for me?" and start asking, "How can I trust and honor him?"

2. The presence that calms our storms

When the disciples saw Jesus walking on water, they were terrified until they heard his voice: "It is I; do not be afraid." That promise still steadies trembling hearts. The same Lord who feeds our hunger also meets us in our storms. His presence doesn't always calm the waves, but it always calms his people. The moment we invite him into the boat, we find ourselves closer to shore than we imagined. Faith doesn't mean escaping the storm—it means trusting the One who walks through it with us. The sea obeyed his feet, and so can our fears.

3. Feed on Christ, not just information about him

Jesus' words about eating his flesh and drinking his blood point to an intimate, ongoing dependence on him. To "feed" on Christ means to make his life our sustenance, his truth our nourishment, his cross our daily bread. Christianity is not a spectator faith but a consuming one. Sermons, songs, and study notes are tools, but they are not the meal. Spiritual starvation often comes not from lack of exposure but from lack of appetite. When we feed on Jesus through trust, obedience, and gratitude, we discover that satisfaction isn't found in what we accumulate but in who abides within us.

4. Stay when others walk away

When the teaching grew hard, the crowd thinned. Following Jesus always tests commitment. The Bread of Life will eventually confront us with truths that challenge pride, comfort, or understanding. Many turned back because they wanted miracles without mystery, blessings without belief. But Peter's words still ring true: "Lord, to whom shall we go? You have the words of eternal life." Real faith matures when we choose to stay even when others leave. Faith that endures doesn't need all the answers—it needs the right allegiance. Sometimes the greatest miracle is simply remaining at his side when walking away would be easier.

CONCLUSION

From hillside feast to hard sayings, John 6 reveals that following Jesus means more than seeking miracles—it means trusting the Messiah. He fed the hungry, calmed the storm, and declared himself the true Bread of Life. Those who stayed discovered that eternal satisfaction comes only through faith in him.

In the next chapter, opposition to Jesus intensifies. As the Feast of Booths approaches, his teaching will divide opinions even further. Some will wonder, some will plot, and others will believe. The Bread of Life who satisfied hunger in Galilee will now confront disbelief in Jerusalem, showing that truth is never neutral—it always demands a decision.

REFLECTION

1. What does the feeding of the five thousand teach you about Jesus' compassion and sufficiency?

2. When have you been tempted to seek Jesus mainly for what he can do, not who he is?

3. How has Jesus met you in "stormy seas" when life felt beyond your control?

4. What does it mean for you personally to "feed" on Christ instead of simply learning about him?

5. Why do you think Jesus let many followers walk away after his hard teaching?

6. What keeps you faithful to Christ when his way feels difficult or confusing?

DISCUSSION

1. Why did Jesus refuse to let the crowd make him king after feeding them?

2. How does the miracle of the loaves point ahead to the meaning of the cross and communion?

3. What does Jesus' walking on water reveal about his identity and presence with his people?

4. In what ways does modern Christianity risk repeating the crowd's mistake—wanting bread without belief?

5. How can we cultivate a daily hunger for Jesus as our true bread of life?

6. How does Peter's confession at the end of the chapter challenge your own commitment to follow?

8

DIVISION & DECISION
JOHN 7

Objective: To recognize Jesus as the source of living water and respond to his invitation with obedient faith.

INTRODUCTION

In 1903, the Wright brothers tested their flying machine on a windy hill in North Carolina. Crowds had doubted them, newspapers ignored them, and even family members were skeptical. But on that December morning, their invention lifted off the ground for twelve seconds that changed history. Timing mattered. They waited until conditions were right—and when the moment came, they rose.

John 7 opens with another moment shaped by divine timing. Jesus' brothers urged him to go public at the Feast of Booths, but he refused to move on their schedule. His mission followed the Father's calendar, not human pressure. When he finally went to Jerusalem, his teaching divided the crowd. Some marveled, others mocked, and the leaders plotted his arrest.

In the midst of confusion and hostility, Jesus stood up and cried out, "If anyone thirsts, let him come to me and drink." Surrounded by religious ritual and spiritual drought, he offered living water to any heart willing to believe.

This lesson reminds us that faith requires patience, humility, and response. God's work unfolds on his timetable, his truth confronts appearances, and his grace quenches every thirst. The invitation is simple but urgent: don't just attend the feast—come and drink.

EXAMINATION
The feast and the Father's timing (7:1-13)
By the time we reach John 7, the atmosphere surrounding Jesus had shifted from curiosity to hostility. The religious leaders were no longer asking questions—they were plotting. Verse 1 opens bluntly: "He would not go about in Judea, because the Jews were seeking to kill him." Yet Jesus' ministry was not driven by fear but by timing. He moved by the Father's calendar, not public demand.

The occasion was the Feast of Booths (or Tabernacles), one of Israel's most joyful festivals. For a week, families lived in makeshift shelters, remembering God's provision during the wilderness wanderings. Each day included water-pouring ceremonies and candle lighting—symbols of God's sustaining presence. Against that backdrop, Jesus would soon reveal himself as both living water and the light of the world.

His brothers urged him to go to Jerusalem publicly: "Show yourself to the world." They were thinking like promoters, not disciples. John makes it clear that they didn't believe in him. Their words sounded supportive, but their motives were sarcastic. "If you're the Messiah," they implied, "prove it."

Jesus replied that his time had not yet come. The world didn't hate his brothers because they blended in, but it hated him because he testified that its works were evil. He would go to the feast, but in his Father's way and on his Father's schedule. He didn't avoid conflict; he avoided premature confrontation.

Later, he went up to Jerusalem quietly, without fanfare. The city buzzed with speculation—some said he was good, others claimed he deceived people. Yet no one spoke openly for fear of the authorities. The silence of the crowd spoke volumes about the climate of fear. Everyone had an opinion; few had courage.

Teaching in the temple (7:14-24)
Halfway through the feast, Jesus appeared in the temple and began to teach. The crowds were astonished: "How is it that this man has learning, when he has never studied?" They assumed authority must come from academia.

Jesus answered, "My teaching is not mine, but his who sent me." His doctrine carried divine origin, not human credentials.

Then he gave a test for discernment: "If anyone's will is to do God's will, he will know whether the teaching is from God." Obedience precedes understanding. Revelation is given to the willing, not the merely curious. Many struggle to grasp spiritual truth not because the Bible is unclear, but because their hearts resist its implications.

Jesus also confronted their hypocrisy. They accused him of breaking the Sabbath when he healed the lame man in John 5, yet they circumcised infants on the Sabbath to keep the law of Moses. "If on the Sabbath a man receives circumcision… are you angry with me because on the Sabbath I made a man's whole body well?" He exposed their inconsistency with a single question. Then he delivered a principle that still rebukes religious superficiality: "Do not judge by appearances, but judge with right judgment."

The crowd looked at externals; Jesus looked at essentials. They obsessed over law codes; he cared about life. The law's purpose was restoration, not regulation—and the Lord of the Sabbath knew that better than anyone.

Division and debate (7:25–36)

The debate deepened. Some Jerusalem residents recognized Jesus and whispered, "Isn't this the man they're trying to kill? Yet here he is, speaking openly." They wondered if the authorities had quietly changed their minds: "Can it be that the rulers really know that this is the Christ?" But then doubt returned. "We know where this man comes from, and when the Christ appears, no one will know where he comes from."

Their reasoning was flawed, and their expectations misguided. They knew Jesus' hometown but not his true origin. He cried out in the temple, "You know me, and you know where I come from. But I have not come of my own accord; he who sent me is true, and him you do not know." His words were a direct claim to divine commissioning—and a direct insult to their supposed knowledge of God.

The crowd's reaction split along predictable lines. Some tried to arrest him, but his hour had not yet come. Others believed, saying, "When the Christ appears, will he do more signs than this man has done?" Belief and unbelief stood side by side in the same temple, listening to the same sermon. The difference wasn't evidence—it was openness.

The Pharisees, hearing whispers of belief, sent officers to arrest Jesus. He told them calmly, "I will be with you a little longer, and then I am going to him who sent me." His mission was nearly complete. They would seek him and not find him, for where he was going they could not come. The leaders puzzled over his words, assuming he meant to travel abroad. They missed the obvious—he was speaking of returning to the Father. The tragedy of spiritual blindness is not lack of intelligence but lack of surrender.

The living water invitation (7:37–39)

On the last and greatest day of the feast, Jesus stood and cried out, "If anyone thirsts, let him come to me and drink." The timing was perfect. During the Feast of Booths, priests would pour out water from the Pool of Siloam at the temple altar, thanking God for rain and recalling the water from the rock in the wilderness. At the exact moment the water-pouring reached its climax, Jesus made his declaration: he himself was the fulfillment of that symbol.

"Whoever believes in me, as the Scripture has said, 'Out of his heart will flow rivers of living water.'" John explains that Jesus was speaking about the Holy Spirit, who would be given after his glorification. The imagery echoes the promise of Ezekiel 47 and Isaiah 44—life flowing from the presence of God to renew a dry land.

The offer was universal—"If anyone thirsts"—and personal—"let him come to me." The world still runs dry at every other well. The crowd had come to Jerusalem to celebrate God's provision in the past; Jesus invited them to experience it in the present.

That invitation remains one of the simplest and most profound in Scripture. He didn't say, "Work harder," or "Learn more," but "Come and drink." Grace is not earned but received. The same Savior who fed hungry bodies now offered to fill thirsty souls.

Reactions and resistance (7:40–52)

The crowd's reaction fractured again. Some said, "This is truly the Prophet." Others declared, "This is the Christ." But others objected: "Is the Christ to come from Galilee? Has not the Scripture said that the Christ comes from Bethlehem, the village where David was?" Ironically, that's exactly where Jesus was born—but their ignorance fed their unbelief. The problem wasn't misinformation; it was unwillingness to investigate truth.

"So there was a division among the people because of him." That line could serve as a summary of the whole chapter—and much of history since. Jesus has always been the great divider of hearts.

The temple officers returned empty-handed. When the chief priests demanded, "Why did you not bring him?" they replied, "No one ever spoke like this man." That unintentional testimony echoed louder than they realized. The leaders sneered, "Have you also been deceived? Have any of the authorities believed in him?" They dismissed the crowd as ignorant, "accursed" people. The arrogance of unbelief was on full display.

Then Nicodemus, who had visited Jesus earlier, spoke up cautiously: "Does our law judge a man without first giving him a hearing and learning what he does?" The others mocked him: "Are you from Galilee too? Search and see that no prophet arises from Galilee." Their contempt drowned out their reason. The men who prided themselves on defending the law broke it with their bias.

By the end of John 7, opinions about Jesus ranged from faith to fury, curiosity to contempt. The chapter began with threats and ends with division, but through it all, Jesus' invitation still stands: If anyone thirsts, come and drink.

APPLICATION

1. Move on God's timing, not everyone else's

Jesus' brothers urged him to prove himself publicly, but he refused to be driven by pressure or pride. His life followed the Father's timetable, not human expectation. Faith means learning the same rhythm—obedience guided by divine purpose rather than popularity. We often rush ahead or lag behind, but Jesus shows that waiting on God's time is never wasted time. True faith trusts that God's "not yet" is as wise as his "now." When we learn to walk in step with him, we find freedom from the world's hurry and peace in his pace.

2. Obedience unlocks understanding

Jesus told the crowd that anyone who truly desired to do God's will would recognize his teaching as divine. Spiritual understanding doesn't come through argument but through alignment. God's truth opens to those who are willing, not just curious. We often ask for clarity while ignoring conviction. If we wait to obey until we understand everything, we'll never move. The clearest path to knowing God's truth is simply doing it. Every act of obedience deepens perception. When the will bows, the mind brightens.

3. Don't judge by appearances

The religious leaders thought they were defending holiness but were actually opposing heaven. They focused on outward conformity and missed inward transformation. Jesus exposed their hypocrisy with one command: "Judge with right judgment." The same warning still applies. It's easy to measure faith by externals—style, background, success—while missing what God values: humility, mercy, and truth. The crowd saw a carpenter from Galilee; heaven saw the Son sent from glory. When we judge rightly, we see people not through our prejudices but through God's purpose.

4. Come, drink, and overflow

When Jesus cried out, "If anyone thirsts, let him come to me and drink," he offered more than relief—he promised renewal. The Spirit's living water not only satisfies but overflows. Believers aren't meant to be reservoirs of grace but rivers of it. The same Spirit who quenches our thirst turns us into conduits of life for others. The invitation still stands for the weary, the restless, and the religiously dry: come and drink. When we come honestly and drink deeply, we discover what the crowd missed—life that doesn't run out when the feast ends.

CONCLUSION

At the Feast of Booths, Jesus revealed that true satisfaction doesn't come from ritual or reputation but from relationship. His words divided the crowds—some mocked, some marveled, a few believed—but his invitation remained open: "If anyone thirsts, let him come to me and drink." The same Savior who moved by divine timing still calls thirsty hearts to come and find life in him.

In the next chapter, that living water will meet human failure face to face. As a woman caught in sin stands before her accusers, Jesus will write grace into the dust and proclaim himself the light of the world. The One who quenches thirst will soon expose darkness and offer mercy that cannot be silenced.

REFLECTION

1. What does Jesus' refusal to go to Jerusalem on his brothers' timetable teach you about waiting on God's timing?

2. How have you seen obedience open your understanding of God's will?

3. When have you been tempted to judge by appearances instead of spiritual discernment?

4. What does Jesus' invitation—"If anyone thirsts, let him come to me and drink"—mean to you personally?

5. How do you see the Spirit's "living water" flowing through your life to bless others?

6. What divisions or misunderstandings about Jesus do you see in our world today, and how can you respond with grace?

DISCUSSION

1. Why do you think Jesus' brothers misunderstood his mission even though they knew him best?

2. How can Christians today stay faithful to God's timing when others push us to act differently?

3. What practical habits help us judge "with right judgment" rather than by appearance or prejudice?

4. How does Jesus' claim to be the source of living water connect to his earlier conversation with the Samaritan woman in John 4?

5. What can we learn from the way Nicodemus cautiously defended Jesus before the hostile council?

6. How does this chapter prepare us for the deeper conflict and clearer self-revelation that follow in John 8?

9

THE LIGHT OF THE WORLD

JOHN 8

Objective: To understand that Jesus, the light of the world, reveals truth, forgives sin, and offers freedom through himself.

INTRODUCTION

During World War II, a small town in England turned off every streetlight to avoid detection by enemy bombers. One night, a single driver ignored the blackout and left his headlights on. The glow revealed not only his own car but also the entire road into the village—making everyone a target. Light is powerful. It guides, but it also exposes.

In John 8, Jesus declared, "I am the light of the world." Before he spoke those words, he shined that light into one of life's darkest corners—a woman caught in adultery, surrounded by men with stones. In her shame, grace triumphed. Then, as Jesus taught in the temple, his light exposed the hypocrisy of religious leaders who prided themselves on knowledge but rejected truth standing before them.

This chapter contrasts freedom and bondage, light and darkness, humility and hostility. The same light that saves the sinner blinds the self-righteous. Jesus offered mercy to the guilty, truth to the confused, and revelation to the resistant—culminating in his bold declaration, "Before Abraham was, I am."

In this lesson, we meet the Christ who stoops to forgive, stands to confront, and shines to reveal. his light still exposes sin, dispels shame, and draws believers into freedom that only truth can bring.

EXAMINATION

The trap and the Teacher (7:53–8:11)

Early in the morning, Jesus returned to the temple, and as usual, a crowd gathered around him. But this day's lesson was interrupted by a mob armed with stones and self-righteousness. The scribes and Pharisees brought a woman caught in adultery and made her stand before the group. Their goal wasn't justice—it was entrapment. They quoted Moses: "Now in the Law, Moses commanded us to stone such women. What do you say?"

The question was designed as a trap. If Jesus said, "Stone her," he would contradict his message of mercy and risk Roman backlash, since only Rome could authorize executions. If he said, "Let her go," he would appear to reject Moses. Either answer seemed fatal.

Jesus bent down and wrote on the ground with his finger. The only recorded act of Jesus writing was done in the dust—a silent sermon to the self-assured. When they kept pressing him, he straightened up and said, "Let him who is without sin among you be the first to throw a stone at her." Then he stooped down again. One by one, the accusers dropped their stones and slipped away, beginning with the oldest. The law had met the Lord.

When the courtyard finally fell silent, Jesus looked up and said, "Woman, where are they? Has no one condemned you?" "No one, Lord," she replied. And Jesus said, "Neither do I condemn you; go, and from now on sin no more." In that single exchange, righteousness and mercy kissed. Jesus did not excuse her sin; he ended her shame. He condemned sin by forgiving the sinner.

The light of the world (8:12–20)

The festival lights of the Feast of Booths had barely faded when Jesus declared, "I am the light of the world. Whoever follows me will not walk in darkness, but will have the light of life." In the temple courts, enormous lamps had burned all night, symbolizing God's guidance through the wilderness. Jesus now claimed to be the true fulfillment of that symbol—the One who illuminates every path and dispels every shadow.

The Pharisees pounced. "You are bearing witness about yourself; your testimony is not true." They demanded validation according to their legal system. Jesus answered that even if he testified alone, his testimony was valid, because he knew both where he came from and where he was going. "You judge according to the flesh; I judge no one," he said, meaning he didn't judge by appearances. When he did judge, it was in perfect harmony with the Father.

Their debate exposed two kinds of blindness—physical sight but spiritual darkness. They claimed to know God but stood unable to recognize him in front of them. Jesus said, "You know neither me nor my Father. If you knew me, you would know my Father also." The claim was staggering: to know God was to know him.

John adds, "No one arrested him, because his hour had not yet come." Light cannot be extinguished before its time.

Truth that sets free (8:21-36)

Jesus' next words unsettled his audience: "I am going away, and you will seek me, and you will die in your sin. Where I am going, you cannot come." They misunderstood, joking that he might kill himself. But his meaning was deadly serious—those who reject him die in their sin. He told them plainly, "You are from below; I am from above. You are of this world; I am not of this world."

He pressed further: "Unless you believe that I am he, you will die in your sins." The phrase "I am he" again echoes the divine name revealed to Moses. Jesus wasn't offering a moral improvement plan but a lifeline of belief. They asked, "Who are you?"—a question that has defined John's entire Gospel.

Jesus warned them that when he was "lifted up"—a reference to his crucifixion—they would finally understand his identity. Even in judgment, revelation would come. Some who heard believed in him, but many still misunderstood the freedom he offered.

To those who did believe, Jesus said, "If you abide in my word, you are truly my disciples, and you will know the truth, and the truth will set you free." They bristled, claiming, "We are offspring of Abraham and have never been enslaved to anyone." Their denial was almost comical, given their history under Egypt, Babylon, and now Rome.

Jesus explained, "Everyone who commits sin is a slave to sin. The slave does not remain in the house forever; the son remains forever. So if the Son sets you free, you will be free indeed." True freedom isn't political or psychological—it's spiritual. The chains he breaks are invisible and unbreakable by any other hand.

False sons and true believers (8:37–47)

Jesus acknowledged their physical descent from Abraham but exposed their spiritual distance from him. "You seek to kill me because my word finds no place in you." Their behavior proved their true lineage. "If you were Abraham's children, you would be doing the works Abraham did." Instead, they were plotting murder against the One who told them the truth.

They protested, "We have one Father—even God." Jesus countered, "If God were your Father, you would love me, for I came from God and I am here." Their rejection of him proved their estrangement from God. Then he spoke words that peeled away all pretense: "You are of your father the devil, and your will is to do your father's desires." The devil has been a liar and murderer from the beginning, and his children share his nature.

Jesus' bluntness might sound harsh, but it was necessary truth. They claimed to defend God's honor while opposing his Son. Their refusal to believe wasn't due to lack of evidence but love of darkness. "Whoever is of God hears the words of God," Jesus said. "The reason you do not hear them is that you are not of God."

In that moment, religion's mask slipped. The most devout men in Jerusalem turned out to be blind to the very God they claimed to serve.

Before Abraham was, "I am" (8:48–59)

Unable to refute Jesus' words, his opponents resorted to insults: "Are we not right in saying that you are a Samaritan and have a demon?" When logic fails, slander begins. Jesus ignored the insult and replied, "I do not have a demon, but I honor my Father, and you dishonor me."

He spoke of eternal life with astonishing authority: "If anyone keeps my word, he will never see death." The crowd erupted in outrage. "Now we know that you have a demon! Abraham died, as did the prophets, yet you say, 'If anyone keeps my word, he will never taste death.' Are you greater than our father Abraham?"

Jesus answered that if he glorified himself, his glory would be nothing, but the Father—whom they claimed to know—glorified him. "Your father Abraham rejoiced that he would see my day; he saw it and was glad." They scoffed, "You are not yet fifty years old, and have you seen Abraham?"

Then Jesus spoke one of the most defining statements in all Scripture: "Truly, truly, I say to you, before Abraham was, I am." The grammar alone was shocking—he didn't say, "I was," but "I am." He was claiming timeless existence, the very name of God revealed in Exodus 3:14. The Word who became flesh spoke the language of eternity.

The response was immediate. They picked up stones to kill him for blasphemy. But Jesus slipped away; his hour had not yet come. The light of the world could not be extinguished by human hands.

APPLICATION

1. Grace that stoops to restore

The woman caught in adultery met truth and mercy in the same person. The Pharisees used her as bait to trap Jesus, but grace turned the trap inside out. He stooped low to write in the dust, reminding us that holiness never hovers above sinners—it bends down to redeem them. Jesus didn't say her sin was excusable; he said it was forgivable. "Neither do I condemn you" is always followed by "Go, and sin no more." His mercy doesn't minimize sin; it transforms hearts. When grace finds us in the dirt, it doesn't leave us there—it raises us to walk in light.

2. Walk in the light, not the shadows

Jesus declared, "I am the light of the world." Light doesn't merely expose—it guides, reveals, and gives life. The religious leaders preferred their darkness because light exposes motives. But those who follow Jesus never walk alone or blind. Discipleship means walking where his light shines, even when it reveals what we'd rather hide. When our paths feel confusing, the problem isn't that God's light has dimmed—it's that we've wandered into the shadows. Following Jesus brings clarity, not comfort; transformation, not just visibility. To walk in the light is to stay near the One who never flickers or fades.

3. Freedom comes from truth, not tradition

The people who argued with Jesus were proud of their religious heritage. "We are Abraham's descendants," they said, but their confidence rested on ancestry, not faith. Jesus cut through that illusion: "Everyone who sins is a slave to sin… but if the Son sets you free, you will be free indeed." True freedom isn't political, emotional, or intellectual—it's spiritual. It begins when truth dismantles our illusions of control. We are never freer than when we surrender to his authority. Religion without relationship chains us to pride; truth frees us to love. The test of liberty isn't how loudly we claim it, but how deeply we live it.

4. Worship the eternal "I Am"

When Jesus said, "Before Abraham was, I am," he revealed his eternal identity. The crowd reached for stones, but faith reaches for worship. The same voice that spoke to Moses from the burning bush now stood in human flesh. The "I Am" who parted seas, guided Israel, and filled the temple had come to walk among his people. Every other light fades, but his still burns unchanging. The only fitting response to the "I Am" is awe and allegiance. If Jesus is who he claimed to be, neutrality isn't an option. The light of the world deserves our trust, our obedience, and our worship—because he alone is God with us.

CONCLUSION

In this chapter, the light of the world stooped low to lift the guilty and stood tall to confront the proud. The woman caught in sin found mercy without compromise, while the self-assured found judgment without repentance. Jesus revealed that real freedom isn't inherited, earned, or deserved—it's received through the Son who sets us free. His declaration, "Before Abraham was, I am," left no room for neutrality. The One who offers forgiveness also demands faith.

In the next chapter, that same light will not only expose but illuminate. A man born blind will see both physically and spiritually, showing that those who admit their blindness can finally behold the glory of God.

REFLECTION

1. What do Jesus' actions toward the woman caught in adultery teach you about his balance of grace and truth?

2. How has the light of Christ exposed or healed hidden areas in your own life?

3. What does it mean for you to "walk in the light" on an ordinary day?

4. How does Jesus' promise that "the truth will set you free" challenge your understanding of real freedom?

5. Why is Jesus' claim, "Before Abraham was, I am," central to your faith?

6. What part of this chapter most strengthens your confidence in Jesus' identity and authority?

DISCUSSION

1. Why do you think Jesus refused to answer the accusers of the adulterous woman directly at first?

2. How can we show both compassion and conviction when confronting sin in others today?

3. What are some practical ways believers can live as "children of light" in a dark culture?

4. How does this chapter redefine the idea of spiritual freedom in contrast to modern definitions?

5. Why do religious people sometimes resist Jesus' truth more than obvious sinners do?

6. How does this passage prepare us for Jesus' next claim, "I am the light of the world," in John 9, where he gives sight to the blind?

10

SEEING & BELIEVING

JOHN 9

Objective: To recognize that Jesus gives true sight—opening eyes, transforming faith, and revealing God's glory through obedience and belief.

INTRODUCTION

In 1725, a young British sailor named John Newton was tossed about in a violent storm at sea. He cried out for mercy, and the ship somehow survived. Years later, after leaving the slave trade and surrendering his life to Christ, Newton wrote the words that would echo for centuries: "I once was lost, but now am found; was blind, but now I see."

John 9 tells the story of another man who could have sung that line. Born blind, he had never seen the sun, the faces of his parents, or the temple he begged beside. Then Jesus came by. With a touch of muddy hands and a word of command, the light of the world gave sight where there had only been darkness. What began as a miracle of healing became a testimony of faith and courage.

As the man's vision sharpened, so did his understanding of who Jesus was. The chapter contrasts his growing faith with the Pharisees' hardening blindness. The man who once begged for coins ended up defending the Savior before scholars.

This lesson reminds us that spiritual sight begins when we admit our blindness. The same Lord who opened one man's eyes still brings light to those humble enough to believe.

EXAMINATION

The man born blind (vv. 1-7)

As Jesus walked along, he saw a man blind from birth. To most people, the man was invisible—a beggar on the roadside, a fixture of misfortune. But Jesus saw him, and that made all the difference. The disciples saw him too, but only as a theological puzzle: "Rabbi, who sinned, this man or his parents, that he was born blind?" Their question reflected a common assumption—that suffering must always trace back to sin. They wanted an explanation; Jesus offered a revelation.

"It was not that this man sinned, or his parents," Jesus said, "but that the works of God might be displayed in him." In other words, his blindness wasn't punishment but platform—a stage on which divine grace would perform. Then Jesus added, "We must work the works of him who sent me while it is day; night is coming, when no one can work." His mission carried urgency. The light of the world was on borrowed time, and every act of mercy was part of his message.

Jesus spat on the ground, made mud with the saliva, and spread it on the man's eyes. The Creator who once formed man from dust now used dust to restore sight. He told him, "Go, wash in the pool of Siloam." The man obeyed, stumbled his way to the water, washed—and came back seeing. One moment, darkness; the next, daylight. The first thing his eyes ever saw was the face of obedience fulfilled.

Questions and quarrels (vv. 8-17)

The healing caused a stir. Neighbors who had long passed the beggar without a second glance now gathered in confusion. "Is this not the man who used to sit and beg?" Some said yes, others argued no—it only looked like him. He settled it himself: "I am the man." When they asked how it happened, he gave a simple testimony: "The man called Jesus made mud, anointed my eyes, and said to me, 'Go to Siloam and wash.' So I went and washed and received my sight."

The crowd brought him to the Pharisees, partly out of curiosity and partly because it was the Sabbath. That detail guaranteed controversy. Jesus had healed—and even made mud—on the Sabbath, which violated their interpretation of rest. The Pharisees interrogated the man, and the debate quickly split the room. Some said, "This man is not from God, for he does not keep the Sabbath." Others asked, "How can a man who is a sinner do such signs?" The division ran deep: law versus love, form versus freedom.

When asked for his opinion, the formerly blind man gave a courageous answer: "He is a prophet." His sight was still new, but his faith was already forming. He didn't yet see Jesus clearly, but he knew enough to speak boldly. The Pharisees, however, were already digging trenches.

Fearful parents and fearless faith (vv. 18-34)

Refusing to believe the man's testimony, the Pharisees summoned his parents. "Is this your son, who you say was born blind? How then does he now see?" They confirmed his identity but distanced themselves from the miracle. "We know that this is our son and that he was born blind. But how he now sees we do not know… Ask him; he is of age." John explains why: they feared the Jews, for anyone who confessed Jesus as the Christ would be cast out of the synagogue.

Fear often silences those who should celebrate. The parents had spent years longing for their son's healing but shrank back from praising the healer. Religious pressure has a way of turning gratitude into caution.

So the leaders called the man back and tried again: "Give glory to God. We know that this man is a sinner." Their verdict came before the evidence. But the man refused to recant. His reply stands among the simplest and strongest confessions in all of Scripture: "Whether he is a sinner I do not know. One thing I do know, that though I was blind, now I see."

His words cut through their arguments like sunlight through fog. When they pressed further—"What did he do to you? How did he open your eyes?"—his wit surfaced: "I have told you already, and you would not listen. Why do you want to hear it again? Do you also want to become his disciples?" That sarcasm cost him dearly. The leaders hurled insults, accused him of following a fraud, and reminded him of their credentials: "We are disciples of Moses."

The man, now bolder than ever, turned theology back on the theologians: "Why, this is an amazing thing! You do not know where he comes from, and yet he opened my eyes." He reasoned that God doesn't listen to sinners, yet this man's prayer had power. "If this man were not from God, he could do nothing." Logic met arrogance—and lost. They expelled him from the synagogue. The man who had spent his life excluded by blindness was now excluded by belief.

True sight and real blindness (vv. 35-41)

When Jesus heard that the man had been cast out, he went looking for him. The shepherd who finds his sheep isn't satisfied with physical healing; he seeks faith. Jesus asked, "Do you believe in the Son of Man?" The man replied, "And who is he, sir, that I may believe in him?" Jesus said, "You have seen him, and it is he who is speaking to you." The man who once couldn't see now beheld the Savior face to face. He said, "Lord, I believe," and worshiped him.

That moment completed his healing. His eyes had opened to light, but now his heart opened to truth. The progression is striking: he first called Jesus "the man," then "a prophet," then "from God," and finally "Lord." Faith is often born in stages, moving from knowledge to conviction to worship.

Jesus then declared the paradox of the gospel: "For judgment I came into this world, that those who do not see may see, and those who see may become blind." The Pharisees nearby took offense: "Are we also blind?" Jesus answered, "If you were blind, you would have no guilt; but now that you say, 'We see,' your guilt remains." Their problem wasn't lack of evidence but refusal to admit need. The man who knew he was blind could see; those who claimed sight stumbled in darkness.

The chapter ends where it began—with blindness and vision, but the roles are reversed. The beggar gained everything and lost nothing; the religious elite lost everything and learned nothing. Jesus proved that he was more than the light of the world—he was the One who gives sight to anyone humble enough to confess their blindness.

APPLICATION

1. When pain becomes a platform

The disciples looked at the blind man and asked, "Who sinned?" Jesus looked and said, "Here's a story where God will shine." The difference between pity and purpose is perspective. Not every hardship is punishment—some are stages for God's glory. The man's blindness became a pulpit for grace. When life leaves us asking why, Jesus often answers with "What now?" He turns setbacks into showcases for his power. Faith learns to see suffering not as wasted time but as divine opportunity. The next time you feel overlooked or misunderstood, remember: the same God who saw a forgotten beggar sees you—and he's not finished writing your story.

2. Obedience before understanding

The blind man didn't know who Jesus was, but he obeyed his command. He stumbled toward Siloam with mud on his face and hope in his heart. Sometimes faith looks foolish until it works. Obedience doesn't always make sense before it acts. We often want full explanations; Jesus asks for full trust. He still tells us, "Go wash," inviting us to believe before we see. The greatest miracles often happen on the other side of obedience. Faith moves feet before it clears up vision. When God calls you to step out into something unclear, remember this man's journey—he didn't argue, analyze, or delay; he simply went and came back seeing.

3. Courage in the face of opposition

The healed man's boldness grew with every question. The more he was pressured, the stronger his faith became. By the end, the once-blind beggar was teaching theology to the theologians. Faith that costs nothing usually changes nothing. True discipleship will face opposition—from culture, religion, or even family—but Christ is worth every risk. The man's parents stayed silent; he spoke. The fear of losing comfort keeps many from confessing Christ, but silence can blind us faster than sin. The world still needs witnesses who can say, "One thing I know—though I was blind, now I see." The credibility of a transformed life outshines the noise of a hostile crowd.

4. Seeing Jesus for who he is

The man's understanding of Jesus deepened until it became worship. That's how sight works—first clarity, then conviction, then adoration. Seeing Jesus clearly always leads to kneeling before him humbly. The Pharisees claimed sight but missed the light; the beggar confessed blindness and found vision. Pride blinds; humility reveals. When we admit our need, Jesus opens our eyes to truth and joy that self-serving religion can't give. The miracle of John 9 isn't just about eyes that worked—it's about a heart that believed. The same Savior still finds outcasts, opens eyes, and calls them to faith. Once grace helps you see him clearly, you'll never mistake another voice for his again.

CONCLUSION

The man born blind received more than sight—he received a Savior. His story moved from darkness to daylight, from confusion to confession, from exclusion to worship. Meanwhile, the Pharisees who claimed to see were exposed as truly blind. Jesus proved that the light of the world still shines brightest in humble hearts that admit their need. The miracle was not just that eyes opened, but that faith awakened.

In the next chapter, Jesus will describe himself as the Good Shepherd who calls his sheep by name. The same voice that said, "Go wash," will now say, "Come follow," leading his people with truth, protection, and love that no blindness or darkness can overcome.

REFLECTION

1. How does Jesus' response to the disciples' question about sin reshape your view of suffering?

2. When have you had to obey God before understanding what he was doing?

3. What part of the healed man's story most strengthens your faith?

4. How have you seen fear silence people who once wanted to speak for Christ?

5. What does this story teach you about the difference between religious pride and humble faith?

6. In what ways has Jesus opened your spiritual eyes to see more clearly who he is?

DISCUSSION

1. Why did Jesus use mud and water to heal the blind man instead of just speaking the miracle?

2. What does the healed man's courage under interrogation teach us about evangelism today?

3. How can Christians respond with both compassion and confidence when facing hostility for their faith?

4. What practical steps help us view trials as opportunities for God's glory rather than punishment?

5. Why do you think the Pharisees became more spiritually blind as the story progressed?

6. How does this miracle prepare us for Jesus' teaching about the Good Shepherd in John 10?

11

THE GOOD SHEPHERD

JOHN 10

Objective: To understand that Jesus, the good shepherd, leads, protects, and gives abundant, eternal life to his sheep.

INTRODUCTION

In 2015, a shepherd in Iceland accidentally left a gate open, and more than a hundred sheep wandered into the fog. Days later, when rescuers tried to gather them, the animals panicked and scattered—until the shepherd called out. At the sound of his voice, every head lifted. The flock turned, bleating in unison, and followed him home. They knew who loved them.

In John 10, Jesus described himself as the Good Shepherd who knows his sheep by name and calls them to life. The image was tender but also confrontational. The religious leaders had just cast out the man born blind, proving themselves to be false shepherds. Now Jesus declared that he alone was the true door to safety and the only shepherd worth following.

This chapter reveals the heart of Christ's leadership. He doesn't coerce; he calls. He doesn't drive from behind; he leads from the front. The Good Shepherd protects, provides, and—most astonishing of all—lays down his life for the sheep. His care is both personal and powerful, his voice both gentle and commanding.

As we study this passage, we'll see that the life Jesus offers is abundant, secure, and guided by the One who never loses a sheep.

EXAMINATION

The true shepherd and the door (10:1–6)

Jesus continued teaching after healing the man born blind, contrasting himself with the false shepherds of Israel. The image of shepherding ran deep in Jewish memory. From Abraham to David to the prophets, shepherds symbolized both leadership and care. Ezekiel 34 had condemned Israel's leaders for feeding themselves instead of their flocks. Against that backdrop, Jesus introduced a parable that was less a cozy metaphor and more a confrontation.

"Truly, truly, I say to you, he who does not enter the sheepfold by the door but climbs in by another way, that man is a thief and a robber." The sheepfold represented the people of God, and Jesus was describing the religious leaders who had seized power for personal gain. The true shepherd enters legitimately, and the gatekeeper opens for him. The sheep recognize his voice and follow because they know him.

John notes that the listeners didn't understand the figure of speech. They were accustomed to teachers who talked about God abstractly; Jesus talked about him relationally. To drive the point home, he explained the imagery more plainly—and personally.

The door of salvation (10:7–10)

"So Jesus again said to them, 'Truly, truly, I say to you, I am the door of the sheep.'" This is the third of John's seven "I am" statements. Shepherds in that time often slept in the entryway of the fold, literally becoming the door—no sheep could leave and no predator could enter except through them. Jesus wasn't describing himself as one of many doors but the only one. "If anyone enters by me, he will be saved and will go in and out and find pasture."

That promise carries both safety and satisfaction. "Go in and out" implies freedom, not confinement. Jesus offers life that is both secure and abundant. He contrasted himself with the impostors: "The thief comes only to steal and kill and destroy. I came that they may have life and have it abundantly."

Abundant life doesn't mean longer years or fuller wallets; it means deeper joy, lasting peace, and restored relationship with God. Every counterfeit shepherd—whether power, success, religion, or self—ultimately steals what it promises to give. Jesus alone leads to life.

The good shepherd (10:11–18)

"I am the good shepherd. The good shepherd lays down his life for the sheep." With that declaration, Jesus moved from protection to sacrifice. The adjective "good" (Greek *kalos*) means not merely "moral" but "noble," "beautiful," and "worthy." The goodness of this shepherd is proven not by charm but by the cross.

The hired hand, he said, works for wages and flees when wolves appear. His concern is comfort, not care. But the good shepherd stays—and bleeds—for his flock. "I know my own and my own know me," Jesus said, "just as the Father knows me and I know the Father." That's an astounding statement. The intimacy between Jesus and his followers mirrors the intimacy between him and the Father—eternal, unbreakable, and full of love.

He also looked beyond Israel: "I have other sheep that are not of this fold. I must bring them also, and they will listen to my voice." This foreshadowed the inclusion of Gentile believers in one united flock. The shepherd's mission was always global, gathering every nation under one call and one cross.

Finally, Jesus declared that his sacrifice would be voluntary: "No one takes it from me, but I lay it down of my own accord. I have authority to lay it down, and I have authority to take it up again." His death would not be a tragedy forced upon him but a triumph freely offered. The cross was not the work of wolves but the will of the shepherd.

Division among the Jews (10:19–21)

When Jesus finished speaking, the crowd fractured again. Some said, "He has a demon, and is insane; why listen to him?" Others reasoned, "These are not the words of one who is oppressed by a demon. Can a demon open the eyes of the blind?" The debate revealed two kinds of hearing: those deafened by pride and those drawn by truth.

Throughout John's Gospel, miracles serve as signs, but signs demanded interpretation. The healing of the blind man in chapter 9 was meant to point to the shepherd in chapter 10. Yet many refused to connect the dots. Light had shone in darkness, and the darkness still tried to argue.

The shepherd and the Father (10:22-30)

Months later, during the Feast of Dedication (Hanukkah), Jesus returned to Jerusalem. The feast celebrated the rededication of the temple after its defilement by foreign rule—ironically, Jesus now stood as the true temple the leaders were rejecting. As he walked in Solomon's portico, the Jews surrounded him: "How long will you keep us in suspense? If you are the Christ, tell us plainly."

Jesus answered, "I told you, and you do not believe. The works that I do in my Father's name bear witness about me." The problem wasn't lack of information; it was lack of faith. "But you do not believe because you are not among my sheep." Belief isn't the cause of belonging—it's the evidence of it.

Then Jesus described the security of his flock with words that have comforted believers for centuries: "My sheep hear my voice, and I know them, and they follow me. I give them eternal life, and they will never perish, and no one will snatch them out of my hand." The same hands that would soon be pierced held his people with unbreakable strength.

He added, "My Father, who has given them to me, is greater than all, and no one is able to snatch them out of the Father's hand. I and the Father are one." That final sentence was not a metaphor—it was a claim of divine equality. The unity between Father and Son ensures the security of every Christian.

Opposition and escape (10:31-42)

The crowd's response was swift: they picked up stones to kill him. Jesus asked, "I have shown you many good works from the Father; for which of them are you going to stone me?" They replied, "It is not for a good work that we are going to stone you but for blasphemy, because you, being a man, make yourself God."

Jesus quoted Psalm 82:6 ("I said, you are gods") to expose their inconsistency. If human judges could be metaphorically called "gods" for carrying divine authority, how much more rightful was his claim as the One sanctified and sent by the Father? "If I am not doing the works of my

Father, then do not believe me," he said. "But if I do them, even though you do not believe me, believe the works."

His appeal was gracious—look at the evidence, even if your heart struggles to believe the messenger. But their rage overcame reason, and they tried to seize him again. He escaped their grasp, crossing the Jordan to the place where John the Baptist had first baptized. There, away from hostility, many came to him and believed. "John did no sign," they said, "but everything that John said about this man was true." The good shepherd continued gathering his flock, one heart at a time.

APPLICATION

1. Follow the shepherd's voice

Sheep recognize their shepherd by sound, not sight. They trust his voice even in confusion or darkness. Jesus said, "My sheep hear my voice, and I know them." The Christian life begins and continues by listening. We live in a world full of competing voices—religion, culture, ego, fear—but the shepherd's call cuts through the noise. We learn his tone through Scripture, prayer, and obedience. The more we listen, the clearer it becomes. True discipleship isn't about mastering theology as much as responding to a Person. The test of hearing his voice is simple: do we follow where he leads, even when the path runs through valleys instead of meadows?

2. Rest in his care

Jesus didn't describe himself as a boss or a general but as a shepherd who knows his sheep by name. That image brings comfort to weary believers who feel forgotten or fragile. Our worth isn't based on our strength but on his care. "He calls his own sheep by name and leads them out." The One who laid down his life also guards our lives. His promise—"No one will snatch them out of my hand"—isn't poetic exaggeration; it's eternal assurance. The grip of grace doesn't slip. When the world feels like a field full of wolves, remember whose hand holds you. The same hand that carries nail scars carries you.

3. Beware of false shepherds

Jesus contrasted his care with the cruelty of thieves and hired hands. False shepherds climb over walls to exploit, not protect. They use people's fears and faith for personal gain. We still see them today—leaders who love control more than compassion, movements that promise freedom but deliver bondage. The best defense against deception is intimacy with the real shepherd. Sheep who stay near his voice won't follow a stranger's. Sound teaching, humble character, and Christ-centered love mark true leadership. When in doubt, ask: does this shepherd reflect the One who lays down his life or the one who takes what isn't his?

4. Live the abundant life

Jesus came not just to save but to satisfy. "I came that they may have life and have it abundantly." That abundance isn't measured in possessions or ease but in presence—his. Abundant life flows from knowing the shepherd, not from escaping the pasture's limits. It's a life marked by peace in turmoil, purpose in work, and joy in obedience. The world offers thrill; Jesus offers wholeness. Every time we trust him instead of ourselves, abundance deepens. The same shepherd who leads us beside still waters also leads us through shadowed valleys—and in both, his goodness follows. The abundant life is not trouble-free; it's shepherd-filled.

CONCLUSION

The good shepherd's voice still calls across every generation—gentle enough to comfort, strong enough to save. Jesus contrasted himself with every false shepherd who exploits the flock. He knows his sheep by name, guards them with unbreakable love, and gives life that no thief can steal. His care doesn't end at the gate—it continues into eternity, secured by the unity of the Father and the Son.

In the next chapter, the shepherd's power over life will be displayed in full. Standing at a friend's tomb, Jesus will call a dead man by name—and the sheep will rise. The One who laid down his life will soon prove he holds the power to give it back.

REFLECTION

1. How does Jesus' description of himself as both the door and the shepherd deepen your understanding of salvation?

2. When have you most clearly recognized the shepherd's voice in your own life?

3. What does it mean to you personally that no one can "snatch" you from his hand?

4. How does Jesus' willingness to lay down his life redefine what true leadership looks like?

5. Where have you seen "thieves and hired hands" trying to steal joy or distort truth in today's world?

6. In what ways has following the shepherd brought abundance—not ease—but deep, sustaining life?

DISCUSSION

1. Why do you think Jesus used shepherd imagery instead of more powerful symbols like kings or warriors?

2. How can believers discern between the voice of the true shepherd and the noise of false shepherds today?

3. What practical habits help Christians grow more sensitive to hearing Jesus' voice daily?

4. How does the promise of eternal security ("no one will snatch them out of my hand") strengthen faith and service?

5. What lessons about leadership and care can churches learn from Jesus' model as the good shepherd?

6. How does this chapter prepare us for Jesus' later claim, "I am the resurrection and the life," in John 11?

12

GLORY THROUGH GRIEF
JOHN 11

Objective: To trust Jesus as the resurrection and the life, who brings glory, hope, and faith through every trial.

INTRODUCTION

In 1963, archaeologists opened an Egyptian tomb that had been sealed for over 3,000 years. Inside were treasures untouched by time—and one tragic symbol: a faded bouquet of flowers, still arranged as if waiting for life that would never return. The ancient world buried its dead with hope, but without assurance.

In John 11, we find a tomb and a hope that refuses to fade. Jesus' friend Lazarus had died, and his sisters, Mary and Martha, wrestled with the same question we still ask: where was God when it mattered most? Jesus' delay seems cruel, but his purpose was glorious. Through their grief, he revealed one of the most breathtaking truths in Scripture: "I am the resurrection and the life."

This chapter reminds us that faith isn't believing God will do what we want, but trusting he knows what's best. Jesus didn't prevent the funeral—he transformed it. His tears at Lazarus's tomb show compassion; his command, "Come out," shows authority.

Here, the power of Jesus over death meets the tenderness of his love for people. The lesson invites us to trust him when life feels late, to believe even when it hurts, and to remember that for those who know the resurrection and the life, death is never the end.

EXAMINATION

The delayed arrival (11:1–16)

The story of Lazarus begins not with tragedy but with love. "Now Jesus loved Martha and her sister and Lazarus." That statement shapes everything that followed. Lazarus's illness was not a sign of neglect but a set-up for glory. When word reached Jesus that his friend was sick, his reply shocked the disciples: "This illness does not lead to death. It is for the glory of God, so that the Son of God may be glorified through it."

Then came the puzzling part—he stayed where he was for two more days. Love delayed. The one who could heal with a word chose to wait. Divine love sometimes moves slower than human panic. God's timing rarely fits our schedule, but it never fails his purpose.

When he finally announced his plan to return to Judea, the disciples protested. The last time he'd been there, the leaders had tried to stone him. "Are you going there again?" they asked. Jesus replied with a cryptic proverb about walking in the daylight—those who walk in obedience don't stumble. His decision wasn't reckless; it was righteous. Then he told them plainly, "Lazarus has died, and for your sake I am glad that I was not there, so that you may believe."

Thomas, ever the realist, muttered, "Let us also go, that we may die with him." It wasn't courage so much as resignation. Yet even in his gloom, he followed. Faith sometimes looks like simply going when you don't understand.

Martha's faith and Jesus' promise (11:17–27)

When Jesus arrived in Bethany, Lazarus had already been in the tomb four days. Jewish custom considered the soul's departure final after three days— Lazarus was beyond all hope. Many friends had come to console Mary and Martha. When Martha heard Jesus was near, she went out to meet him; Mary stayed behind.

"Lord," Martha said, "if you had been here, my brother would not have died." There's no accusation in her tone, only grief mingled with faith. "But even now I know that whatever you ask from God, God will give you." She believed in his power, if not yet in his timing.

Jesus told her, "Your brother will rise again." Martha nodded, assuming he meant the resurrection at the end of time. Jesus answered with one of the most profound declarations in Scripture: "I am the resurrection and the life. Whoever believes in me, though he die, yet shall he live, and everyone who lives and believes in me shall never die."

He didn't just promise resurrection—he embodied it. Life wasn't a future event but a present reality in him. Death bows not to doctrine but to a Person. Then came the question that every believer must answer: "Do you believe this?" Martha replied with remarkable clarity, "Yes, Lord; I believe that you are the Christ, the Son of God, who is coming into the world."

Her faith wasn't flawless, but it was firm. She couldn't see how Jesus would act, but she trusted who he was. Sometimes that's all faith can do—cling to identity when answers are unclear.

Mary's tears and Jesus' anger (11:28–37)

Martha returned home and called her sister. "The Teacher is here and is calling for you." Mary rose quickly and went to him. When she reached Jesus, she fell at his feet and echoed her sister's lament: "Lord, if you had been here, my brother would not have died."

Seeing her weeping—and the mourners beside her—Jesus was "deeply moved in his spirit and greatly troubled." The Greek term conveys more than sympathy; it suggests indignation, even anger. He wasn't frustrated with Mary but with death itself—the enemy that stalks every human story. Compassion filled his heart, but holy fury stirred his soul.

"Where have you laid him?" he asked. They said, "Lord, come and see." Then John recorded the shortest and one of the most powerful verses in Scripture: "Jesus wept."

Those tears weren't weakness; God incarnate stood beside a tomb and wept—not because he lacked power, but because he felt pain. He enters our sorrow before erasing it. The crowd drew mixed conclusions. Some said, "See how he loved him." Others sneered, "Could not he who opened the eyes of the blind also have kept this man from dying?" Even miracles can't silence cynicism.

The miracle at the tomb (11:38-44)

Jesus came to the tomb, a cave sealed with a stone. "Take away the stone," he commanded. Martha hesitated. "Lord, by this time there will be an odor, for he has been dead four days." Faith flickered but fear spoke louder. Jesus replied gently, "Did I not tell you that if you believed you would see the glory of God?"

They took away the stone. Jesus lifted his eyes and prayed aloud—not because the Father needed to hear, but because the crowd needed to. "Father, I thank you that you have heard me. I knew that you always hear me, but I said this on account of the people standing around, that they may believe that you sent me."

Then he cried out with a loud voice, "Lazarus, come out!" Augustine once remarked that if Jesus hadn't named Lazarus specifically, every corpse in the world would have walked out! The man who had died emerged, his hands and feet bound with linen strips, his face wrapped with a cloth. Jesus said, "Unbind him, and let him go."

What had been a funeral became a festival. Grief turned to glory, mourning to marvel. Lazarus walked out of death because the Word of Life called him by name.

The consequences of glory (11:45-57)

The miracle set off a chain reaction. Many who saw believed in Jesus, but others ran to the Pharisees to report what had happened. The chief priests convened the Sanhedrin: "What are we to do? For this man performs many signs. If we let him go on like this, everyone will believe in him, and the Romans will come and take away both our place and our nation."

Their concern wasn't theology—it was control. Caiaphas, the high priest, spoke with chilling irony: "It is better for you that one man should die for the people, not that the whole nation should perish." John explains that Caiaphas, without realizing it, had prophesied the gospel. The substitution he meant politically would soon be fulfilled spiritually.

From that day on, they plotted to kill Jesus. The raising of Lazarus, meant to display glory, sealed the decision to crucify the one who gave it. Light had shone in darkness, and darkness struck back.

Jesus withdrew with his disciples to Ephraim, near the wilderness. The Passover approached, and the leaders' command went out: anyone who knew his whereabouts should report it. Death was hunting the life-giver, but his hour had not yet come.

The chapter that began with sickness ends with a death warrant—but also with resurrection life breaking through the grave. Lazarus's tomb foreshadowed another one soon to open, proving once and for all that the resurrection and the life is not an event but a person who still calls our names.

APPLICATION

1. When God waits, he's still working

Jesus' delay in coming to Bethany puzzled everyone. If he loved Lazarus, why wait? Yet every hour of silence was a stroke in a larger masterpiece. God's timing rarely matches our urgency, but it always matches his glory. Sometimes his greatest miracles come after we think it's too late. Waiting seasons stretch faith and teach trust. When God seems absent, he's arranging something deeper than relief—revelation. The tomb wasn't proof of neglect but the stage for resurrection. Faith learns to say, "Even now I know," like Martha—believing that Jesus' love and power are never in conflict, even when we don't understand his timing.

2. Bring your tears to the One who weeps

Jesus' tears at Lazarus' tomb remind us that divine compassion feels human pain. The Son of God didn't stand apart from grief—he entered it. When we cry, we never cry alone. He joins us in sorrow before he turns it into joy. His anger at death assures us that our pain matters and that he intends to destroy what destroys us. Sometimes believers think faith forbids emotion, but John 11 shows that tears are sacred when shed in the presence of hope. When you can't stop weeping, remember—he wept too. The God who grieves with you also raises what feels lost beyond recovery.

3. Believe beyond the tomb

Jesus' words to Martha—"I am the resurrection and the life"—still echo through every graveyard of despair. Resurrection isn't only a future event; it's a present relationship. Believers don't just await eternal life—they already share it through him. Even death can't interrupt that connection. Faith doesn't deny the reality of death but defies its finality. When Jesus called Lazarus by name, he proved that death can't silence those he loves. Every Christian will one day hear the same summons: "Come out." Until then, our hope isn't that life will never hurt but that it will never end. The resurrection life begins now and continues forever in his presence.

4. Let God's glory rewrite your story

What began as heartbreak became a headline for God's glory. Martha and Mary didn't know their tears would testify for centuries. The same is true for us. God often uses our hardest seasons as the clearest mirrors of his power. Like Lazarus, we become living proof that Jesus turns graves into grace. But resurrection also carries responsibility—Lazarus had to walk out, and others had to unbind him. When God brings new life, we can't stay wrapped in the old. Every miracle invites movement, every deliverance demands discipleship. The God who calls us out of death also calls us forward into light, free and unbound for his glory.

CONCLUSION

In Bethany, Jesus revealed that death is not the end for those who believe in him. His delay tested faith, his tears showed compassion, and his command—"Lazarus, come out!"—proved his authority over the grave. The one who wept with mourners also called life from death, turning sorrow into praise. Every detail of this miracle pointed forward to his own resurrection, where he would defeat death once and for all.

In the next chapter, that victory begins to take shape as Mary anoints Jesus for burial and the cross draws near. The one who raised the dead will soon walk toward his own tomb—so he can open ours forever.

REFLECTION

1. When has God's timing in your life felt like a delay, and how did you see his purpose later?

2. What does Jesus' weeping at Lazarus' tomb reveal about his heart for human pain?

3. How does Jesus' statement, "I am the resurrection and the life," reshape your view of death and eternity?

4. What does this story teach you about believing even when you don't understand?

5. Where might God be inviting you to "roll away the stone" of fear or unbelief?

6. How can your own story—of loss, waiting, or redemption—bring glory to God like Lazarus's did?

DISCUSSION

1. Why do you think Jesus delayed going to Bethany when he could have healed Lazarus immediately?

2. How can believers balance grief and faith when facing suffering or death?

3. What do Martha and Mary's different reactions to Jesus teach us about faith under pressure?

4. How does this miracle reveal both Jesus' humanity and his divinity?

5. In what ways does Lazarus's story foreshadow Jesus' own death and resurrection?

6. What steps can we take to live out resurrection life now, not just after death?

13

THE HOUR HAS COME

JOHN 12

Objective: To understand that Jesus' "hour" reveals God's glory through humility, sacrifice, and the call to follow him in faith.

INTRODUCTION

In 1992, a young musician named Jeff Buckley performed a quiet, unadvertised concert in a New York café. Only a handful of people were there, but word of that performance spread far and wide. Years later, his voice became legendary. What began as a small moment of beauty turned into something that echoed far beyond the room.

John 12 opens with a similar scene. In a quiet home in Bethany, Mary of Bethany broke open an alabaster jar and filled the air with devotion. That fragrance reached far beyond the room—it pointed to the cross. From there, Jesus entered Jerusalem to the shouts of "Hosanna," welcomed as a king yet destined to die as a lamb. The crowds misunderstood his mission, but heaven did not. The hour had come—the moment all history had been moving toward.

This chapter stands at the hinge of John's Gospel, where public ministry gives way to the path of sacrifice. Here, worship meets betrayal, faith meets fear, and life is found through death. Jesus revealed that true glory doesn't come from avoiding suffering but from redeeming it. His journey to the cross was not tragedy—it was triumph, the seed of eternal life for all who believe.

EXAMINATION

Mary's costly devotion (12:1-11)

Six days before the Passover, Jesus returned to Bethany, the village of his friends. It was a gathering of gratitude—Lazarus sat at the table alive again, Martha served as she always did, and Mary did what she did best: she worshiped. Taking a pound of pure nard, a costly perfume imported from India, she poured it on Jesus' feet and wiped them with her hair. The fragrance filled the house, a fitting image of how true worship lingers long after the act itself.

Judas Iscariot immediately objected: "Why was this ointment not sold for three hundred denarii and given to the poor?" John reveals his hypocrisy—Judas didn't care about the poor; he was a thief. Jesus defended Mary's act as prophetic: "Leave her alone, so that she may keep it for the day of my burial." Her gift was extravagant but appropriate—what she poured out in life would soon anoint him in death.

Mary's devotion contrasted sharply with Judas's deceit. Her sacrifice smelled of love; his greed reeked of betrayal. The same aroma that honored Jesus filled the room and offended the proud. Genuine worship always does both.

Meanwhile, the chief priests plotted to kill not only Jesus but Lazarus too, since his resurrection had drawn many Jews to faith. The one who embodied life now had death warrants written against him—and anyone who reminded others of his power.

The triumphal entry (12:12-19)

The next day, the crowds swelled as pilgrims poured into Jerusalem for the Passover. Hearing that Jesus was coming, they took palm branches—a national symbol of victory—and went out to meet him, shouting, "Hosanna! Blessed is he who comes in the name of the Lord, even the King of Israel!"

It looked like triumph, but it was misunderstood triumph. Jesus entered not on a warhorse but on a young donkey, fulfilling Zechariah 9:9: "Fear not, daughter of Zion; behold, your king is coming, sitting on a donkey's colt." His entrance declared both kingship and humility. The Messiah came not to conquer Rome but to conquer sin.

John notes that even the disciples didn't understand these things at first. Only after Jesus was glorified did they realize how the Scriptures had been fulfilled. The Pharisees, watching the cheering crowds, muttered in frustration, "You see that you are gaining nothing. Look, the world has gone after him." Their sarcasm was truer than they knew. Many in the world would soon follow—not in political rebellion, but in faith.

This scene marked the high point of public enthusiasm and the beginning of the final descent toward the cross. The same voices crying "Hosanna" would soon cry "Crucify." Humanity's praise is fickle, but Jesus' purpose is steadfast.

The Greeks seek Jesus (12:20–36)

Among the festival pilgrims were some Greeks—Gentile God-fearers who came to worship. They approached Philip with a simple request: "Sir, we wish to see Jesus." Their arrival signaled a turning point. The gospel that began with Jewish shepherds at Bethlehem was now reaching Gentile seekers in Jerusalem.

Philip told Andrew, and together they told Jesus. His response didn't sound like a direct answer but revealed divine timing: "The hour has come for the Son of Man to be glorified." Up to this point in John's Gospel, Jesus has repeatedly said his hour had not yet come. Now, as the cross loomed, he declared that it had. The arrival of the nations meant his mission was ready to bear fruit for the world.

Then Jesus spoke of the paradox of glory through death: "Truly, truly, I say to you, unless a grain of wheat falls into the earth and dies, it remains alone; but if it dies, it bears much fruit." He described his own sacrifice as a seed planted in the soil of suffering to produce life for others. To follow him means the same—losing life to gain it.

His soul was troubled, yet he refused to pray for escape. "Father, glorify your name," he said. A voice thundered from heaven, "I have glorified it, and I will glorify it again." The crowd heard it and argued whether it was thunder or an angel. Jesus explained that the voice came not for his sake but for theirs: "Now is the judgment of this world; now will the ruler of this world be cast out."

He then spoke the heart of the gospel: "And I, when I am lifted up from the earth, will draw all people to myself." "Lifted up" pointed to both crucifixion and exaltation. The cross would become the magnet of grace, pulling every heart willing to believe.

The crowd was confused. "We have heard that the Christ remains forever. How can you say that the Son of Man must be lifted up?" Jesus urged them to walk in the light while they still had it, warning that darkness was coming. When he finished speaking, he withdrew and hid himself. The light of the world would soon be eclipsed by a cross.

The tragedy of unbelief (12:37–43)

Despite all the miracles—water to wine, blind eyes opened, dead raised—many still refused to believe. John quoted Isaiah: "Lord, who has believed what he heard from us? And to whom has the arm of the Lord been revealed?" Their unbelief wasn't new; it fulfilled prophecy. Isaiah had seen the glory of the Lord and written that God had "blinded their eyes and hardened their hearts." This wasn't divine cruelty but human consequence—persistent rejection leading to spiritual callousness.

Some rulers did believe, but they kept silent for fear of being put out of the synagogue. "They loved the glory that comes from man more than the glory that comes from God." The contrast is heartbreaking: Mary had poured out perfume publicly; these men hid their faith privately. Courageous devotion gave way to cautious diplomacy. Fear remains one of faith's fiercest enemies.

Unbelief doesn't always look like defiance; sometimes it looks like silence. The tragedy of John 12 isn't just those who opposed Jesus—it's those who believed but were too afraid to say so.

The final appeal (12:44–50)

John closes Jesus' public ministry with a final invitation. Jesus cried out, summarizing his mission: "Whoever believes in me, believes not in me but in him who sent me." He came as light to dispel darkness, not as judge but as Savior. Yet those who rejected him would face judgment—not from his lips, but from the word they ignored.

"For I have not spoken on my own authority," he said, "but the Father who sent me has himself given me a commandment—what to say and what to speak. And I know that his commandment is eternal life." Every word Jesus spoke was the Father's call to life. Rejecting him wasn't just dismissing a teacher; it was turning away from God's final offer of salvation.

The chapter—and Jesus' public ministry—ended with both invitation and warning. The light of the world had shone brightly, but many chose blindness. His miracles had proven power; his words had revealed love. Now, with his hour arrived, the world's salvation hung in the balance.

APPLICATION

1. Worship that costs something

Mary's act of devotion filled the room with fragrance, but it also emptied her savings. Genuine worship always costs something—time, pride, comfort, or control. Her example reminds us that love for Jesus is never wasted, even when others misunderstand it. Judas saw waste; Jesus saw worth. When we give freely to Christ, heaven calls it beautiful. True disciples don't ask, "How much can I keep?" but "How much can I give?" Faith that costs nothing means nothing. Our devotion should fill the room—not with performance, but with presence. The fragrance of love lingers far longer than the applause of onlookers.

2. Following a humble King

When Jesus rode into Jerusalem on a donkey, he displayed power through humility. The crowds wanted a revolutionary; he came as a redeemer. His kingdom advances not through force but through surrender. In a world that celebrates dominance, Jesus still calls us to humility. He rules hearts, not armies; he conquers pride, not nations. Following this King means embracing the paradox of victory through suffering and service. Like the disciples, we may not understand his ways at first, but the Spirit helps us see that every step of humility leads closer to glory. When we follow a lowly King, we learn that greatness always rides on gentleness.

3. Dying to bear fruit

Jesus taught that a grain of wheat must die to bear fruit. The principle applies to every disciple: life grows through surrender, not self-preservation. We often pray for fruitfulness without embracing the process of being buried—surrendering our plans, comfort, or pride. But resurrection life always follows crucified living. Every loss laid at Jesus' feet becomes seed for something greater. The path of obedience may look like decline, but it's actually increase. The world measures success by survival; the cross measures it by sacrifice. When we let go for Christ's sake, we don't lose—we multiply.

4. Walk in the light while you can

Jesus warned the crowd to walk in the light before darkness overtook them. The same urgency applies today. Spiritual light is a privilege, not a guarantee. Every time we hear truth and ignore it, our hearts grow dimmer. Faith isn't merely about understanding—it's about responding while grace still calls. The tragedy of John 12 is not ignorance but indifference. Many saw miracles and turned away. The longer we delay obedience, the easier it becomes to stay in the shadows. Today's light is tomorrow's memory if we don't walk in it. The call of Christ remains urgent and clear: "Believe in the light, that you may become sons of light."

CONCLUSION

In John 12, the spotlight of history turned toward the cross. Mary's worship prepared Jesus for burial, the crowds hailed a King they didn't understand, and Jesus declared that his hour had finally come. Through a grain of wheat falling into the ground, he revealed that life would bloom through death. The glory of God would shine brightest through a crucified Savior.

As this chapter ends, Jesus' public ministry closes with one last invitation: to walk in the light while there's still time. In the next chapter, that light moves into an upper room, where the King will kneel like a servant and wash the feet of those he came to save.

REFLECTION

1. What does Mary's act of worship teach you about loving Jesus with sacrifice, not convenience?

2. How does Jesus' humility in the triumphal entry challenge your understanding of leadership and power?

3. What does it mean for you personally to be a "grain of wheat" that dies to bear fruit?

4. Where do you sense Jesus inviting you to walk in his light rather than stay in comfort or fear?

5. How do the reactions of the crowd and religious leaders warn us against spiritual apathy?

6. What encourages you most about Jesus' words, "And I, when I am lifted up, will draw all people to myself"?

DISCUSSION

1. Why do you think Mary's devotion pleased Jesus but irritated Judas?

2. How does the triumphal entry reveal both the glory and the misunderstanding of Jesus' mission?

3. What does Jesus' response to the Greeks show about his global purpose and the meaning of his "hour"?

4. How can Christians today live out the principle of "losing life to find it"?

5. Why is unbelief often rooted in fear of people's opinions rather than lack of evidence?

6. How does this chapter prepare us for the events of John 13–17, where Jesus turns from public signs to private preparation?

www.ingramcontent.com/pod-product-compliance
Lightning Source LLC
Chambersburg PA
CBHW060336050426
42449CB00011B/2775